SHARIN

Rita F. Snowden i... countries and is th... books for adults and children. After six years at business she trained as a deaconess of the New Zealand Methodist Church, serving in turn two pioneer country areas before moving to the largest city for several years of social work during an economic depression.

Miss Snowden has served the world Church, beyond her own denomination, with regular broadcasting commitments. She has written and spoken in Britain, Canada, the United States, in Australia, and in Tonga at the invitation of Queen Salote. She has represented her church at the World Methodist Conference in Oxford; later being elected the first woman Vice-President of the New Zealand Methodist Church, and President of its Deaconess Association. She has been an Honorary Vice-President of the New Zealand Women Writers' Society, and is a Fellow of the International Institute of Arts and Letters, and a member of P.E.N.

Miss Snowden has been honoured by the award of the Order of the British Empire, and by the citation of "The Upper Room" in America.

Her most recent books are *Prayers for Busy People, Christianity Close to Life, Bedtime Stories and Prayers* (for children), *I Believe Here and Now, Discoveries That Delight, Further Good News, Continually Aware, Good Company, Prayers in Large Print, Like Wind on the Grasses, Secrets, People and Places* and *A Good Harvest*.

Books by the same author
available in Fount Paperbacks

Bedtime Stories and Prayers
(for children)
Continually Aware
Discoveries That Delight
Further Good News
Good Company
A Good Harvest
I Believe Here and Now
Like Wind on the Grasses
More Prayers for Women
People and Places
Prayers in Large Print
Secrets
A Woman's Book of Prayers

Rita Snowden also edited
In the Hands of God
by William Barclay

Rita F. Snowden

SHARING SURPRISES

Collins
FOUNT PAPERBACKS

First published in Great Britain by Fount Paperbacks, London
in 1989

Copyright © Rita F. Snowden 1989

Printed and bound in Great Britain by
William Collins Sons & Co. Ltd, Glasgow

CONDITIONS OF SALE

This book is sold subject to the condition
that it shall not, by way of trade or otherwise,
be lent, re-sold, hired out or otherwise circulated
without the publisher's prior consent in any form of
binding or cover other than that in which it is
published and without a similar condition
including this condition being imposed
on the subsequent purchaser

*Gladly Dedicated to "M"
in Edinburgh,
with On-going Gratitude*

CONTENTS

INTRODUCTION	9
A Young Life Re-made	15
Everything or Nothing	20
Gifts of Gratitude!	24
A Picnic Surprise	28
Love Upon Its Knees	32
My Young Helper	37
Like the Master	41
Our Christmas Adoration	45
Greed Goes Against Life	49
Set to Washing Up	53
As the Years Pass	57
Taking Levels	61
Easter Memories	65
On the Lake's Rim	69
A Surprise One Season	73
His Footprints	77
Personal and Precious	81
God's Point of View	85
Beauty We Must Have	89
A Woman of Words	93
A Well-Earned Name	97

Wool-Gathering	101
Endless Caring	105
Surprises at Work	110
A Gift of Love	114
Courage – and Compassion	118
One Needs to Know	122
With Great Spirit	126
The Best of Things	130
In His World	134
ACKNOWLEDGEMENTS	140

INTRODUCTION

There is no saying how early the seed of a book is sown in an author's heart and mind. In this case it was its title, and the lasting importance of its contents: **Surprises**!

As a subject, it's in no sense limited to childhood – though I early learned, riding my cycle to and from school – that when Surprise drops out of life, it's like a puncture – leaving one "riding on the rims"!

And that's no fun – and life was never meant to be that! So, from the start, I've set out to share **Surprises** where I can – and that has brought me joy! And not me only!

* * *

I set off from home one evening, not long ago, to speak to a gathering in a fine Salvation Army Hall on the uplands, a few miles off. I had been guest speaker there before, and this time, had decided to speak to them about **Surprises**! (There are a number in the New Testament that I thought would be good to share – but little did I think that one awaited *me* there – and before I could say a word!)

The charming young Captain who chaired the meeting had only just come back by plane from a world gathering in London. But before she left – already packed, soon to be off – somebody gave her a copy

Sharing Surprises

of the Salvation Army newspaper, *The War Cry*. Having her hands full with travel documents, and other esssentials for home, she tucked it into and then locked her case, already "tagged" for the other side of the world.

In time – air weary – she was met by her family, both sides having lots to tell. Later, getting down to her unpacking, she came upon her *War Cry*, but did not stop to look through it then as there were things to put away, and things to prepare for the next few days, not least, a big gathering, with a guest speaker. When she did open the paper, there facing her was a pleasant photograph of a Salvation Army "lass" taken at the time she had been interviewed for the paper. And underneath her picture was the question she had been asked at the time: "ARE YOU THE REAL RITA SNOWDEN?"

"Well," she was reported to have answered, "I'm real enough to myself – and to many others – but I know what you mean. *I read her books, too.*"

* * *

Now standing by my side, as I waited to speak, the young Captain, with a chuckle, held up her copy of *The War Cry*, and read aloud to all its interview of the young unknown "lassie"!

My subject – Surprises – had already been announced, but I had to wait till the happy barrage of laughter subsided. (And a pair of scissors was found, enabling me to return home that night with the cutting.) And next morning I wrote off to my young namesake pictured there!

Introduction

Very soon, I had a letter back, telling me how she "loved" my books, and also telling me a little about her own work, for the Master we both "*rejoice to serve*"!

However many and varied the themes presented in that Hall in the future, I am told those kindly folk "will never forget the night Sister Rita Snowden, the author, spoke about **Surprises**!" And I'll never forget it, myself.

But when things settled, I was able to pass on to them the good news of the coming Christ Child – *and the Surprise that was*! First, to Mary, then to Joseph the carpenter – and soon to all! Into the simple chosen town of Bethlehem, "a Little Child brought Light – so that never again, in man's realm of the Spirit, can it be utter night!"

* * *

From His Babyhood and Childhood, we moved out with Him, into His manly ministry of *surprising* outreach and compassion – typified in His talk *with* the woman at the well-side at Sychar, whom others only "*spoke about*"! She had a bad reputation, so she came to draw water at the well at midday, under the broiling sun when nobody was about. But this day, it was different. (John 4:4.)

But when the disciples returned from buying food in the village, Moffatt's version of the gospel story says: "They were *surprised* that *He was talking with a woman*." And he might have added, "Such a woman!"

Still, it was not beyond the mercy of Christ!

Sharing Surprises

* * *

And following on with the sad story of the Cross – yet another **Surprise** awaited. News of His death spread – and His close disciples were utterly cast down.

> And when all the crowds who had collected for the sight saw what had happened, [according to Dr Luke's Gospel record chapter 23:48, Moffatt's New Testament, once more] they turned away beating their breasts. As for His acquaintances, they were all standing at a distance to look on, with the women who had accompanied Him from Galilee.
> Now there was a man called Joseph, a member of council but a good and just man who had not voted for their plan of action; he belonged to Arimathea, a Jewish town, and he was on the outlook for the Reign of God. This Joseph went to Pilate and asked him for the body of Jesus. He then took it down, wrapped it in linen, and put it in a tomb cut out of the rock where no one had yet been buried.
> It was the day of the Preparation and the sabbath was just dawning; so the women who had accompanied Him from Galilee and who had followed Joseph noted the tomb and the position of the body, and then they went home, to prepare spices and perfumes.
> On the sabbath they rested, in obedience

Introduction

to God's command, *but on the first day of the week at early dawn* [the Gospel says] they took the spices they had prepared and went to the tomb.

And we all know, now, what awaited them there! Telling of it later – and now reported in that same chapter, Luke 24, where we have the much loved record of the two, who, heavy-hearted, set off home to Emmaus, and on the way met up with another traveller, to whom they told their experience in the city, adding, "Though some women of our number *gave us a surprise*; they were at the tomb early in the morning and could not find His body, but they came to tell us that they had actually seen a vision of angels who declared He was alive. Some of our company did go to the tomb and found things exactly as the women had said." (Moffatt's rendering of Luke 24 to verse 24, and especially verse 22.) *For no other faithful women in all time have found themselves entrusted with a greater surprise*!

Now let us tell it out – and not only once a year, at Easter! The year round, let us rejoice in these SURPRISES!

POSTCRIPT
I find pleasure in recalling that nearer our own time – actually between 1332 and 1400 – keenly observant William Langland wrote of "a fair field of folk ... *working and wondering*".

So I think of you, my readers of this book, and set

Sharing Surprises

at the end of each chapter a special section marked WORKING AND WONDERING, for you to fill out in your Quiet Time. I hope you will welcome it.

R.F.S.

A Young Life Re-made

Long ago now, at the end of a lengthy illness, I filled my convalescence with writing a book – putting a little of my personality – body, mind and spirit – between two covers. My very first, of many!

And it brought me a **wonderful surprise**. The little book, made up of a collection of eager letters between one young woman and another, was titled *Through Open Windows*, as a great number of older readers still remember. And its jacket, which I drew, showed a young woman looking out through an open window. Below I set four challenging lines in print:

> Stretch out your hand and take the world's wide gift
> Of joy and beauty . . .
> Open the windows of your wondering heart
> To God's supreme creation! Anon.

The young woman of my drawing did exactly that! We never had the pleasure of meeting, though I wish we had! And after ten years, her minister, looking back, wrote to me:

> There are times when even the most optimistic of us get an attack of the "blues". I thought I would like to send you this remarkable account of a transformed life. Dorothy

grew up with an elder brother and younger sister, and lacked nothing. Fond of reading, she had musical tastes, and was skilled at hand-work. She was tall, and was more than passably good looking. But up to reaching twenty-one, she seemed aloof in the home, and even less easily approached by any outside the family.

After a three-year absence ... I received a message telling of her death. On arrival at the parents' home I found a large company assembled; some had come long distances. The boy scouts formed a guard of honour. There were more people outside the church than the number of those able to gain admission. My absence left me at a complete loss to account for the demonstration of affection, at the passing of such a reserved young woman. Later, in the home, in conversation with Dorothy's mother, I made an effort to unravel the mystery.

Her mother, without a word, took a homemade picture from the wall. It showed a young woman sitting at an open window – a copy of the author's frontispiece of *Through Open Windows*, and its verse underneath. In the interval of years the miracle had happened. A new spirit had come to Dorothy; the icy cold reserve had been banished; life had begun anew. Work in the Church, and teaching in the Sunday school. The boy scouts had found a godmother in Dorothy, as with full heart and soul, she entered into all

A Young Life Re-made

the worthwhile activities of the community.
If your book [added the minister] *has done no
more than this, how worthwhile it has been.*

Dorothy's copy of my frontispiece now hangs in the Church she came to love, beside her plaque of remembrance, as I have been taken to see, when visiting the township!

Working and Wondering

"We have acquaintances, and casual friends – but few of us enjoy intimate life-changing relationships that last", says one anonymous writer. *Is that so?*

Rebecca West, the distinguished author, said, "There is a definite process by which one makes people into friends, and it involves talking to them [or even the writing of a book] and listening to them for hours at a time."

PRAYER
>"Grant, O Lord, that none may love Thee less this day because of me.
>That never word or act of mine may turn one soul from Thee.

Sharing Surprises

And more daring, yet one other grace would
  I implore –
That many souls this day, because of me, may
  love Thee more."

Anon - a Medieval Petition

Friendship adds a brighter radiance to prosperity, and lightens the burdens of adversity, by dividing and sharing it.

Cicero

MORNING MEDITATION
  Not to the wise, O Lord, not to the prudent,
    Dost Thou reveal Thyself, nor to the art
  Of the logician keen, and coldly student,
    But to the patience of the pure in heart.
  Low is the lintel of Thy truth, and lowly
    Mortals must bend who fain would see Thy
      face;
  Slow from the darkness dawns the day, and
    slowly
    Sinners ascend into Thy dwelling-place.

Unknown

THANKSGIVING
  Eternal God, revealed in Jesus Christ, I rejoice
    in Thy holy Love.
  Let the surprising wonder of that Love, come
    home to me afresh this day.

A Young Life Re-made

Let me learn from life's varied experiences, Thy lasting values.
And accept my deep thanks for the hours when I live richly. Amen.

R.F.S.

Everything or Nothing

A few mornings back, coming from the baker's with my fresh brown loaf, I chanced on a neighbour and her house guest. Set on the same errand, they'd come by way of the beach, but seven minutes' walk from my home, and beautiful and fresh at that early hour!

My neighbour introduced me, and when the newcomer learned that I was an author of many books, she asked what I wrote about. Before I could draw breath, my neighbour herself answered: "*Oh, everything*! I wouldn't be surprised, if it came to it, to find her writing interestingly about '*Nothing*'." We all laughed at that!

But I came home thinking about it. *Nothing* is interesting, isn't it? – especially to those of us who are Christian in this fascinating world! I'd planned a morning's gardening before I went out, and now I got down to it – with a patch of weeding that had been waiting. As I worked, my thoughts turned to Job's words about this self-same world of God's creating.

I've been nine times round it – by ship and by plane – but I've never borrowed Job's words before. Now, a respectable morning's gardening done, I want to get to my writing, with thoughts of some of this world's "natural wonders" I've seen. I shall not be able to mention them all, so many and varied are they. There was little Alice Springs under the quiet

Everything or Nothing

sky affording me the company of Aboriginals I was called to address, singing and listening to me, a thousand miles from the sea!

And there another time, was the place where I stood, by day, on a memorable visit, where America and Canada share in the unimaginable roaring beauty of Niagara Falls! Night and day, for hundreds of years, without a pause – millions of gallons of water have been pouring over, undiminished! *Part of God's world*, created by the lasting One, of things great and small: Everest, up-raised in the sky, snow-crowned – and the tiny, perfect, pearly fingernails of a babe. Rivers and lakes, and silvery-spangled cobweb caught in the morning's light! The Moon, where men have come to walk, marvelling – and the miracle-beauty of countless creatures photographed in the bottom of ocean pools! This is the work of Him, of Whom one said, *"He stretcheth out the north over the empty place, and hangeth the Earth on nothing!"* (Job 26:7; A.V.).

I can't think of anything more surprising!

At least, that is, until I come to the New Testament truth offered us Christians. Paul expressed it superbly, in what is now known to us as Romans 8:38 and 39 (in The New English Bible):

> I am convinced there is *nothing* in *death* or *life*, in the realm of spirits . . . in the world as it is or the world as it shall be, in the forces of the universe, in heights or depths – *nothing in all creation that can separate us from the love of God in Christ Jesus our Lord.*

Sharing Surprises

Working and Wondering

Accept me in my golden time,
  In my dear joys have part!
For Thee the glory of my prime,
  The fullness of my heart!

I cannot, Lord, too early take
  This covenant divine;
Or e'er the happy heart may break
  Whose earliest love was Thine!

Author Unknown

We preach not ourselves, but Christ Jesus the Lord; and ourselves as your servants for Jesus's sake.

For God, who commandeth the light to shine out of darkness, hath shined in our hearts, to give the light of the knowledge of the glory of God in the face of Jesus Christ.

2 Corinthians 4:5–6; A.V.

Our spiritual life is the only precious thing we possess. It is that without which all else is dust and ashes. It is that without which, in spite of all our academic knowledge, we shall become, in St Paul's own words, as sounding brass or as a tinkling cymbal. But it is such a fragile thing, and it is so easily quenched. In the bustle and

Everything or Nothing

hurry of the world's business, you will find that it is threatened with extinction on every side. As Jesus Himself said, "the cares of this world, and the deceitfulness of riches, and the lusts of other things entering in", are always threatening to choke it.

Dr John Baillie in *Christian Devotion*

PRAYER

> Dear Master, in Whose life I see
> All that I would, but fail to be,
> Let Thy clear light for ever shine,
> To shame and guide this life of mine. Amen.

John Hunter

Gifts of Gratitude!

There are words that come alive, aren't there, as we walk through the world! And I love them. Surprisingly, one of my best-loved does not appear in my treasured Authorized Version of the Bible, though it's in a number of our newer versions, as, for instance, in Moffatt: 2 Samuel 16:4; and in the Revised Standard Version: Acts 24:3. These refer to personalities little known: the first, to *Ziba*, thought to have been a servant, recorded as saying: "I bow in humble **gratitude**!" The second, a New Testament character, *Felix*, Governor of Samaria, who on a meaningful occasion is reported to have said: "we accept this with all *gratitude*."

* * *

And two surprise experiences have shown me this same fine word in use amongst people, as I've moved about. The first was in England, or in "the Old Country", as people now living here in New Zealand, but born there, like to call it.

I was in London once, on "The World Day of Prayer" for all Christians, and able to worship in Chelsea Old Church, where, to my joy, I learned of the gratitude of Richard Guildford. It was registered, actually, at my very feet, in the pew where I unknowingly chose to sit. "Long ago", I learned before leaving, "Richard Guildford, on one of the

24

Gifts of Gratitude

unforgettable days of his life, *had made his way to this very church, to meet his bride!*"

This was the reason for the beautifully-stitched "prayer kneeler" at my feet, for during his lifetime, the bridegroom of long ago had arranged for *A gift of Gratitude to God* to be offered through the Old Church – and to *be made for ever, on the regular return of that blessed wedding date*!

(It would come to me, as yet another *surprise*, to learn of other grateful souls, happy to adopt Richard's long-tested expression of Gratitude! There may already be some in your church and in mine, though I have not heard of them. And there has been plenty of time: Richard's dates were in the sixteen-hundreds!)

* * *

A while ago, tying both sides of the world together in gratitude, a **surprise** greeted me in Tonga. I was there as guest-speaker to the Queen's people for some weeks. One of her distinguished Christian leaders, the scholar, Dr Amanaki Havea, drove me, in a Mission Land-Rover, to a distant speaking engagement. And at the end of our homeward drive, as he drew the key from the dashboard, I said: "I heard a story about you today – that when, on a first visit to England, you stepped ashore at Southampton, *you took the sandals from off your feet!*" "Yes," he replied, softly-spoken, "*I did*. It was to me 'holy ground', whence came long ago *all our missionaries, transforming this land* – and I had to speak my gratitude!"

Working and Wondering

PRAYER

Gracious God, I would not take any of the treasurable things of my life for granted.
I rejoice in the dawn that issues in each day – and its promises, and surprises.
For changing seasons, and the beauty of the world, I bless Thee – and for sight and sound, and the capability to walk about.
More than for these good things, I bless Thee for family and friends, showing love and support.
And now day by day, let me never fail to show gratitude for worship, and for fellowship in my church.
For Christ's sake. Amen.

R.F.S.

In the glad morning of my day,
My life to give, my vows to pay –
With no reserve, and no delay,
With all my heart, I come!

Marianne Farningham

Oh God, Source of all light and healing, change with the brightness of Thy Love –

The red of our anger,
The orange of hesitation,
The yellow of cowardice,

Gifts of Gratitude

The green of ignorance,
The blue of depression,
The indigo of unbelief,
The violet of mourning –

so that our human weakness may be transformed into the rainbow's splendour, bringing the beauty of Heaven to us on Earth – through Thy Love. Amen.

Cecil Hunt

Show us how to seek Peace, and pursue it, O God; of whatever colour or clime, we are all Thy children.
Bless our relationships – in our homes, and in schools, and places of work.
Keep us grateful for things commonly enjoyed – books and music, Art and Scripture!
Bless all who struggle in this life – and all who find that daily friendship, and rewards, pass them by.
Strengthen the frail, comfort and heal the sick, we pray –
in the Name of the lastingly, Compassionate Christ. Amen.

R.F.S

A Picnic Surprise

Again and again, during childhood and growing up, leisure was sprinkled with picnics for some of us. And great fun they were! But the surprise of some, I admit, fell well outside the planning.

A friend assured me of this – when she and her missionary husband, serving in Fiji, had the pleasure of welcoming to the Indian Mission in Navua the General Secretary for Overseas Missions. On a certain day – as arranged – the party set off down the coast in the Mission cutter.

All went well until the host – not knowing that the "food box" had been somehow overlooked – asked the distinguished guest whether he would like a cup of tea. "Yes," he replied, without a second thought, "I would!" The sea air had given most aboard a thirst, so the "house boy" was sent below to prepare it. Soon the primus was lit, and the water nearly boiled. But then the boy, surprisingly, put his head out of the cabin where he'd been busy only to say: "*Sa sega, Saka na sucu.*" (There is no milk, sir.) This sad news was passed on to the guest; who with good grace agreed to drink tea *without* milk!

A few minutes later, a sense of expectation was interrupted by a second appearance of the boy, to report: "*Sa sega, Saka na suka.*" (Sir, we have no sugar.) This was also communicated to their guest, who, by

A Picnic Surprise

this time, was really ready for his tea – without milk or sugar!

The primus was still heard buzzing merrily: another minute passed; then the boy appeared a third time, only to report, in a dejected voice, "*Sa sega, Saka na Ti.*" (Sir, we have no tea.)

"At least," commented my friend, "he was tactful, and kept the worst news till last!" But no one aboard will *ever forget that particular picnic*! (Neither shall I – nor how my friend laughed so heartily about it!)

And to this day, whenever I find myself guest at a picnic, it has remained top of my uneasy mind!

For, from that day to this, it's still clear, just as my friend summed it up, unforgettably, in four short, simple words: "No Tea without Tea!"

* * *

In a more serious vein, I now find myself writing **"There is no Forgiveness without Forgiveness"**. Without that Fijian picnic story, I would never have dreamed of putting it like this but it's true, isn't it! "The Lord's Prayer", used more often by us than any other, the world round, leaves us in no doubt about that! It reaches us, as the *only petition* in that lovely prayer, with a condition set!

Without our daily readiness to offer forgiveness to others about us, in this world of our living, *how can God offer us His All-enveloping Forgiveness*? It's a tremendous truth: "*Without forgiveness, there is no Forgiveness!*"

Sharing Surprises

Working and Wondering

Following the cry for bread – within The Lord's Prayer – comes this cry for Forgiveness. And how right the link is! For what is bread for the body, if the spirit is estranged?

R.F.S. in *The Lord's Prayer: The Living Word*,
p.50; Epworth Press

"I remember a girl writing me from abroad", said Florence Allshorn, that lovely spirit of our day, "telling me how thrilled she was over giving a set of lessons on The Lord's Prayer; and the rest of her letter was spent in blackguarding a certain person with whom she was working. And I thought: 'What will she do – what will she do – when she comes to "forgive us our trespasses as we forgive them that trespass against us"?' I felt frightened, for I knew she would somehow . . . do it."

> 'Tis sweet to stammer one letter
> Of the Eternal's language on earth;
> It is called *"forgiveness"*

Anon

Forgiveness is the act by which God brings us back, one by one, whatever the offence, unto a *right* relationship with Himself, and with our fellow men.

R.F.S. in *Discoveries that Delight*, p.134.

A Picnic Surprise

The rubble and wooden debris about the floor had already been gathered, and a plan was being made to sow a short lawn of grass there. The remains of the altar window stood silhouetted against the sky. But even more telling was the Coventry Cross – the cross of silver-plated nails, standing against a great cross made of two charred beams. And below there stood, chiselled deep into the sanctuary stone, two words: FATHER FORGIVE. Just two words – but they were the words of Jesus on His Cross, words that no one standing where I stood in Coventry, could ever forget.

R.F.S.

Lord Christ, Whose Love for sinful men asked forgiveness even for those who nailed Thee to the Cross, give us grace to forget the petty insults we sometimes endure; to overlook the snubs, and to disregard the slights of our unthinking friends . . . So may we be made ready to pray for God's forgiveness of the wrongs we ourselves have inflicted. Amen.

Anon

Love Upon Its Knees

Dr Harry Fosdick is not thinking of a young man before his lady love, when he coins our title for today, but rather of beautiful *Unselfishness in Prayer*. Many, up through the long years, have experienced it, though it is generally called "Intercession". Yet we get over-used to that – and our title is more striking. Paul's embracement of it has long been before us in the New Testament (Romans 15:30):

> "I beseech you, brethren, for the Lord Jesus Christ's sake, and for love of the Spirit, that ye strive together with me in your prayers to God for me."

Or, as the New English Bible puts it:

> "I implore you by our Lord Jesus Christ and for the love that the Spirit inspires, be my allies in the fight."

And Paul keeps it up, writing to his friends in Corinth:

> "From such mortal peril God delivered us; and He will deliver us again, He on whom our hope is fixed ... *if you will co-operate by praying for us*" (2 Corinthians 1:11: N.E.B.)

And again, in 1 Thessalonians 5:25; A.V.: *"Brethren,*

pray for us." Even the New English Bible can't say it more plainly, although J.B. Phillips's words today sound closer to our ears: *"Here you can join in and help by praying for us."*

And this eager intercessory prayer is as beautifully effective today – embracing those whom we love who are in special need, in sorrow, sickness, bewilderment or loneliness.

But it doesn't mean our just mouthing names, as faceless as those crowded into the anonymity of the telephone directory. No! These for whom we pray are loved. They were loved of God our Father, long before ever we knew them, and they are loved by Him still! This is not a mere verbal formality – this is Love that goes deep!

God taught us, through Christ, to think, and pray, in every daily situation. He knows what is happening, just as well as we do. *"Our Father . . . our daily bread . . . our sins"* came as naturally with Him as within our earth relationships. We are bound together in the inescapable, mysterious bundle of Life. Fatherhood is not to be linked with choice or favouritism – God the Creator has made His world on *a family basis*. It is He whose **Love** wants the best for His family; whose **Wisdom** knows the best for all; and whose **Power** can provide the best!

Intercession – above all, prayer – is an expression of this beautiful reality. To lay hold of this "togetherness" is to know a very rich experience. To borrow the words of Evelyn Underhill, a very practical, sensitive Christian of our day, is to claim: "From the greatest disclosure of beauty, to the smallest appeal of Love, from our happiness, to utmost grief, will either

Sharing Surprises

hallow, or not hallow His Name, and *this is the only thing that matters about it.*"

So let us learn the meaning of "Love upon its knees!"

Working and Wondering

Gracious God, our Father, bless this day all who link their prayers, and their lives, in labour to lighten the lot of others.

Let the sacredness of life here come home afresh to me this day.

I bless Thee that I am allowed to live in Thy universe. Greater than Thy Majesty is Thy Love, more lasting than all is Thy Mercy.

Let me this day, I pray, do my ordinary work, as it comes, honestly and gladly, as in Thy presence. Amen.

R.F.S.

Our Master's words – recorded now in Matthew 6:14; R.S.V. – are:

"Beware of practising your piety before men in order to be seen by them; for then you will have no reward from your Father who is in heaven. Thus, when you give alms, sound no trumpet before you, as the hypocrites do in the synagogues and in the streets, that they may be praised by men. Truly, I say to you, they have received their reward. But when you give alms, do not let your left hand know what your right hand is doing, so that your alms may be in secret; and your Father who sees in secret will reward you."

O that men would praise the Lord for His goodness, and for His wonderful works to the children of men!

Psalm 107:31

This is a piece too fair
To be the child of Chance, and not of Care.
No Atoms casually together hurl'd
Could e'er produce so beautiful a world.

John Dryden

You are a child of the Universe, no less than the trees and stars: you have a right to be here. And whether or not it is clear to you . . . Therefore be at peace with God.

Found in Old Saint Paul's Anglican Church
in Baltimore, 1692

Sharing Surprises

"I am aware", says Angela Morgan, "of the splendour that ties
All the things of the Earth with the things of the Skies;
Here in my body, the heavenly heat –
Here in my flesh the melodious beat
Of the planets that circle Divinity's feet –
As I sit quietly here in my chair –
I am aware."

My Young Helper

I was surprised at what the post brought, after I had been so long at my desk, working away. Days merged into weeks, weeks into months, which is normal enough in the making of a book. But in one sense, this one was different! Apart from carefully chosen words it was to have twenty-one beautiful pictures, plucked for my purpose from a succession of world journeys. Its title was settled. It was to be: *While the Candle Burns*.

I reached a point where there remained nothing further to do, save find a suitable picture for the opening study: "Togetherness"! But nowhere could I find it, though for a whole year I had known what I wanted. Then God sent me a young helper, by way of an unknown photographer in a distant city, and before the year was out, my devotional book was finished – and published in London! But it was years before I learned *how*, and then a letter *carrying a surprise* came one morning! The young woman who wrote it said:

> "I worked for an architect at the time. Occasionally, I used to go to the office of a firm, to get prints made for our work. And one day, as I waited, the photographer asked me to look up; and then, to kindly move my head. Soon he was explaining – a photograph was

needed by the author, Rita F. Snowden. It was for a chapter on 'Togetherness', in a new book waiting. It was to show a young couple, much of an age. They were to be coming up a hill, hands linked – the girl, a little in front, setting the pace. Overhead, there would be clouds – but lighted – and the light would be *in their faces*!

"Next", the letter went on, "he called in a young man, a member of staff. And in time, the picture was finished – and sent off to the publishers in London!

"After quite a time", she continued, "stocks of the book came out to New Zealand booksellers – and I got one. I loved it for years", her letter went on. "Then, during an upheaval in moving, it got lost. I was upset. Then, by chance, I heard the author being interviewed on the radio. So I decided to get her address, and write to see if it were possible to get a fresh copy. She got me one – and I was so glad." (It was a well-kept second-hand copy, for postwar paper restrictions were still on.)

I wrote, by return mail – *touched* by her joy, myself glad to learn how she had been "used" to produce the attractive picture in my book so many years before!

* * *

Long, long before that, St Paul, I knew from my New Testament reading, had a "loved" helper who

My Young Helper

left Paul so full of gratitude that he wrote a letter, (now in Romans 16:9; A.V.) "Salute Urbane *our helper in Christ!*"

Was he also young? I've wondered ever since. I've not been able to learn anything more of him. All I can say, understandably, is **"God be praised!"**

Working and Wondering

PRAYER

Eternal God, I give thanks for friends firmly depended on through the years, in my moments of need. And for the many who, one by one – though unknown – are my helpers.

Let those of us blessed with work of our own choosing, use our awareness of others' needs, this day, to Thine honour and glory.

Deliver us from the selfish tyranny of trifles – and let us serve a wider horizon, affecting our fellow men and women helpfully. Amen.

R.F.S.

PSALM

> It is good to give thanks to the Lord,
>   for His love endures for ever.

Wool-Gathering

When in my distress I called to the Lord,
   His answer was to set me free;
The Lord is on my side, I have no fear;

The Lord is on my side, *He is my helper*!

Psalm 118:1,5,7; N.E.B.

**Master, this day –
Take my hands and let them move
At the impulse of Thy Love!**

He comes to us as One unknown, without a name, as of old by the lakeside He came to those men who knew Him not. He speaks to us the same words, **"Follow thou Me"**, and sets us to the task which He has to fulfil for our time. He commands. And to those who obey Him, whether they be wise or simple, He will reveal Himself ... *and as an ineffable mystery, they shall learn in their own experience Who He is.*

Dr Albert Schweitzer

Was it those years in Nazareth
   That trained Thee for Thy Father's will?
And wast Thou never tired to death
   And yet obliged to labour still?

Lord, when our daily job appears
   Too great a burden to be stood,
Remind us of those thirty years –
   And Thy divine apprenticehood.

Anon

Like the Master

Each time I pull open the cutlery drawer in my little kitchen, to prepare a meal for myself or for guests, the name "Sheffield" is before me. It's on each dinner knife there! For seven centuries, and more, knife-blades have issued from that great steel city.

It's some years since my church publishers first sent me to Sheffield on a lecturing tour, and, when it was over, invited me to join a goodly company for an historic moment in "Paradise Square". A *surprise event*!

On another weekday – the 15th of July 1778 – John Wesley himself had come there, to preach to a large crowd! And here were we, *on another weekday* 15th of July – a hundred-and-seventy years later! Our privilege was to dedicate a neat slab, with lettering to explain, along with a very attractive likeness of the little man himself. My view on that day of the crowd was obscured; so in a day or two, I went back again alone – or so I thought. Rain, in drizzling showers, was a feature of that day, the Square enclosed in tall dim buildings, the pavement wet and uneven. I was joined presently by a little old shambling passer-by, in a cloth cap. When he saw the centre of my interest, he made but one comment: "Ah, John Wesley – *he done a lot of good*!" And he meant that as a tribute in the best sense. It was said of Wesley's Master and

Sharing Surprises

Lord, *"He went about doing good"* (Acts 10:58; A.V.).

In our day, a fellow Christian of ours – the Japanese, Kagawa – wrote:

> I read
> In a book
> That a Man called
> CHRIST
> *Went about doing good.*
> It is very disconcerting
> To me
> That I am so easily
> Satisfied
> With just
> Going about!

Such, alas, are "drones" in the closest dictionary definition – "persons who live off the work of others". Unfortunately, every Christian congregation is likely to know one or two. Their name comes from those bees belonging to an ordinary hive, *that bring in no honey*!

And there is as likely to be, where we are, another group akin to them – the "*do-gooders*"! These are busy enough; but what they do adds up to very little in the gracious, ageless, life of the Kingdom of our Lord! (To my surprise, I find them also defined in my same new dictionary, as "drones". Spiritless! Self-pleasing! Sad!) But day by day, we may as likely give thanks for those who, like John Wesley, "*Do good, in the lively, lasting manner of their Lord!*"

Like the Master

Working and Wondering

Says the Psalmist in early times: "Give thanks to the Eternal – *he is good*, his kindness never fails!"

Psalm 107:1; Moffatt

And the New Testament has hardly begun before one man wonders about a good deed. Moffatt says so; very strikingly: Up came a man and said to him, "Teacher, *what good must I do* to gain life eternal?"

Matthew 19:16.

"My Modern-day Prayer" runs like this –

> Here, amid the scramble of
> Time,
> Let me know the Good
> Values
> Of the Kingdom of God
> on Earth!
>
> Here, where politicians lay
> plans;
> Let God's still, small Voice
> be now heard;
> *And His Will be done amongst
> us.* Amen.

R.F.S.

Sharing Surprises

So shalt thou be with power endued
> *From Him Who went about*
The Syrian hillsides *doing good*,
> And casting demons out.

Poet Whittier

So do I rejoice to sing with yet another:

> Direct, control, suggest this day
> All I design, or do, or say,
> That all my powers, with all my might,
> In Thy sole glory may unite.

Hymn

> Saviour, to Thee my soul looks up,
>   My present Saviour, Thou!
> In all the confidence of Hope,
>   I claim the blessing *now*.

Charles Wesley

Our Christmas Adoration

I can't remember which of my early Christmases it was, when I first heard of Raphael. I was shown the likeness of the famous Italian painter on a card which came through the post, and I liked the soft sound of his name, as I still do. I learned that he was born in a home where his father worked as a painter, though he was never as famous as his young son was to become. That was in Urbino, in the border lands of Tuscany and Umbria. (Pretty names for places, I thought – and hoped that when I grew big, I'd go and see them.)

Within the card, I was reminded, Christmas after Christmas, a beautiful painting showed Mary and the Child Jesus. Nobody now knows for sure who painted it – the father or his son. It's just one of the things we can't be sure about.

But of all the sure things, the one I like most is of the times when young Raphael, by then grown up, used to pay a visit to a special friend of his. And if it chanced that the friend was out when he called, Raphael did one surprising thing each time: he *drew a circle on his friend's doorstep*! He didn't need to do more. Nobody could draw a perfect circle like Raphael could! He had no use for a calling-card.

* * *

Nor has any one of us, to keep our Christmas

perfectly. I find myself inspired by this little story, standing as I do on "the doorstep of the world, *pursing my lips to a perfect O of Adoration*"! But I am immensely happier than Raphael – because never, whenever I call, is my Divine, eternally loving Friend absent!

In this gracious experience of Adoration, just now, I come both to receive, and to give! "Adoration", to use the words of the beloved writer, Dr Olive Wyon, a modern saint, "is not primarily a sentiment or a thought. It is *a recognition of the fact that God has laid His hand upon us* . . . In the depth of our being; it is a word which is greater and more absolute than we can ever imagine!"

That is the true meaning of the *Incarnation*, once-and-for-all in this Earth home where we stand meanwhile, at Christmas, with the Adoration we offer.

And the words that rise in our hearts, to sing at this Season, are "Joyful and Triumphant . . ."

> Jesus to Thee be glory given.
> Word of the Father,
> Now in flesh appearing:
> O come, *let us Adore Him,*
> *Christ, the Lord!*

Our Christmas Adoration

Working and Wondering

Bless me now, O Lord, as I ponder others' words:

> When the Christmas candles are burned out;
> The carols have died away;
> The star is set;
> All the radiant song-filled night is past;
> *Thou alone, the Eternal, remainest*; and Thou art enough.
> Remain in me, more beautiful,
> More beloved,
> More real than any of the romance
> That clusters around Thy birthday.

Anon

The God Who rules this earth,
gave life to every race;
He chose its day of birth,
the colour of its face;
So none may claim superior grade
within the family He has made.

Richard G. Jones

The God Who had such heart for us
as made Him leave His house
come down through archipelagos
of stars, and live with us,
has such a store of joys laid down,
their savours will not sour;
the cool gold wines of Paradise,
the bread of heaven's flour.

Sharing Surprises

He'll meet the soul *which comes in love*,
and deal it joy on joy
as once He dealt out star on star
to garrison the sky,
to stand there over rains and snows
and deck the dark of night;
so God will deal the soul, like stars
delight upon delight!

Robert Farren

Greed Goes Against Life

All my school days, along with my country friends, over the miles I walked from home, I carried a pack of sandwiches for lunch. And I never dreamed there was anything more to know about them.

So a surprise awaited me!

As a young woman in my middle twenties, my school days long over, I walked with a companion round the south of England, each carrying a haversack. And there, of a sudden, we came on the little shore town of "Sandwich". We'd never heard of it until that moment!

That morning, on our way as usual, we had come across a tiny grocer's shop that looked able to supply our needs – a small brown loaf, butter, and a few slithers of cooked ham. All too soon, it came time for us to seek out a shady tree on the road's grassy verge.

We learned that at one time, the interesting old town, with its drawbridge, had really been by the sea. For a very long time, its curfew had been rung from St Peter's Church, requiring all and sundry to put out their lights at an agreed hour, since home-made candles with flickering wicks, and lamps, many without glass shades, could so easily topple over. As many of the houses were then wooden they were likely to take fire. Besides that possibility, ships from strange ports came in to the little harbour, and nobody knew,

Sharing Surprises

when night came, what mischief their crews might be up to.

The old town had some attractive, story-book houses, huddled together in a row on each side of its street, some with quaint crooked windows, and roofs that allowed them to lean across, like old gossipy women. And there were a number of other features to explore. But the most notable character had been "The greedy old Earl of Sandwich", away back in the days of King George the Third. He was a great gambler and greedy for gain – as gamblers, in the very nature of things, are – so he was loth to spare so much as a moment of extra time in eating a set meal. So he devised a scheme of taking his meat between two pieces of bread. This allowed him to keep on at his gambling, and eat at the same time.

He was such a greedy old fellow, it seemed, not only greedy for food; but greedy for gain of many kinds – for time, for sport, for praise, for clothes, for possessions, as much as for first place everywhere. Greed shows itself in so many ways. There is, I found, after I'd been "eating sandwiches in Sandwich", a verse in the Bible which says, underlining the misery that greed spells out: "He that is *greedy of gain*, troubleth his own house!" (Proverbs 15:27).

And it's true, isn't it?

Greed Goes Against Life

Working and Wondering

The proverb-maker gives us an additional word:

> "Life thrives like a tree on generosity, but *grasping greed* is death to man."
>
> Proverbs 2:30; Moffatt

And again, Moffatt renders a verse in Psalm 69:13:

> "I pray to Thee, in *Thy great generosity*, O God, *'do Thou accept me'*."

> "He coveteth *greedily* all the day long; but the righteous *giveth and spareth not*."
>
> Proverbs 21:26, A.V.

"Teach us, good Lord," pleads Ignatius Loyola, "to serve Thee *as Thou deserveth* . . . knowing that we do Thy will."

PRAYER
And teach us, O God, to be generous, not only with things but with our thoughts.

R.F.S.

Oh, the comfort, the inexpressible comfort of feeling safe with a person, having neither to weigh

Sharing Surprises

thoughts, nor measure words, but pour them all right out as they are, chaff and grain together, knowing that a faithful hand will take and sift them, keep what is worth keeping and then with the breath of kindness blow the rest away.

George Eliot

You give out little when you give of *your possessions*. It is when you give of yourself that you truly give.

Unknown

How rarely we weigh our neighbours in the same balance in which we weigh ourselves.

Thomas à Kempis

It is impossible to over-emphasize the immense need men have to be really listened to, to be taken seriously, to be understood . . . *No one* can develop freely in this world . . . without feeling understood by at least one person.

Paul Tournier

Set to Washing Up

Washing up is not one of life's events expected to hold surprises. The only one I can remember was not my own – but the newspaper account of Princess Anne, set to washing up at Benenden School. And that's some time ago now. But it made news to headline round the world: a Princess, at her boarding school, sleeping in a dormitory, making her bed, and occasionally at weekends having a turn at the washing up. (But few of us commoners, I imagine, failed to notice it was only once a week, at most; *not three times a day, for evermore*. Approach it as we may, we find there is something in washing up stubbornly routine.)

The average British housewife, I read lately, in the opinion of a Gas Council Home Service Officer, washes up an acre of crockery every year, made up of 18,615 dirty dishes. It's easy to join the realist who wrote: "Ten thousand times I've done my best – and all's to do again." It's hard to lift any routine task to a higher plane; though we're told of Brother Lawrence, a saint of earlier days, who found spirituality (which he called "Practising the Presence of God") among "the clutter of plates" as really as "when kneeling at the blessed sacrament". (But we're not all saints.)

Another approach to this never very exciting routine is that of the artist, Burne-Jones, as Mrs Thirkell, his granddaughter, tells us. Living in the spacious

Sharing Surprises

days of scullery maids, he did what he could for those involved in the unwelcome task of washing up. He fitted one of his own beautiful windows of the Holy Grail over the sink, where the dishes had daily to be dealt with. (But again, stained glass windows are not the possession of many of us.)

A pleasant glimpse of a tree, a patch of blue sky, or a garden, over a modern sink – when the window is not steamed up – can help, it's true, to remind one that life here is not all washing up. There are, thanks be to God, daily, large, beautiful realities to be embraced! A daily reading of selected Scripture can help; and a few morning moments of meditation in silence won't be a wasted experience.

And, I have myself discovered in the average good bookshop today, many a lively devotional guide – many a one, as a paperback, cheaply priced – *from some long-time experienced Christian, very close to earth*!

There is no need to leave our lives dominated by a sink of soapy water – we have here, more resources than that – more strength of character. Royal personages or commoners, we each have routine tasks to deal with. I'm not tempted to declare them unreal – they are indeed real – and daily with us! I do not, in any sense, join the great American preacher William Lyon Phelps, in talking about "the excitement of routine". My prayer is "Father, let me see the difference between the really big, and the little things – and daily keep my spirit from courting pity! In the service of Christ's Kingdom. Amen."

Set to Washing Up

Working and Wondering

God is reminding us constantly that there are types of work that must be done again and again. Some, we think of as commonplace. Is any work that is done with the right spirit, commonplace?

The old Greeks pictured their deities as living on a distant Olympus, quaffing their nectar, pursuing their own pleasures, aloof – unconcerned about the affairs of men. But the words of Jesus are, "*My Father worketh hitherto, and I work*" (John 5:17; A.V.)

Why is our work so important to Him? Is it because our Lord wants it – or because He wants us?

Or possibly, both?

Eyebrows were raised in our time, on hearing Dr William Temple, Archbishop of Canterbury, say: "It is a mistake to think that God is interested solely in religion. Yes, it is surely true that God's purposes in this world are forwarded not only by hassocks and hymn books, by preachers and poor boxes – though surely these are important. House-painters are part of His plan as well as preachers, cooks as well as choir members, drain diggers as well as youth directors."

William Temple's words challenged me one day, as I came from Charing Cross Undergound Station, along the Thames Embankment. There I came upon

Sharing Surprises

a *surprise discovery* – a plaque, set to mark the work of one of God's helpers: *"Sir Joseph Bazalgette, C.B., Engineer of the London Main Drainage System."*

At one time, plague ravaged the city, carrying off countless men and women to their deaths. Devout souls gathered in churches to pray. Little did they know that God was preparing *an answer to their prayers*, in the person of a master drain digger!

Our young Lord was not play acting at the carpenter's bench in little Nazareth. He was actually earning a living – *serving the needs of the community* – as did many another there.

"And what was done in the Carpenter's workshop", one of our day, Evelyn Underhill, is remembered to have said, *"can be done anywhere*. In the engineer's shop, too." And you, and I, can put our place of business in the list. And at day's beginning, pray this little prayer – as sincerely as you do anything each day:

> Son of the Carpenter, receive
> This humble work of mine;
> Worth to my meanest labour give,
> By joining it to Thine! Amen.

As the Years Pass

"Postie" has a share in a good many of the "surprises" that come my way!

"As long as there are postmen," said William James, of an earlier century, "life will have *zest*!" So I feel too! And the term "postmen" of course embraces "postwomen" as it has done now for a long time. And still, from time to time, one comes to my letter box with a handful of letters.

On one of my early English journeys I came upon a tribute to a former postwoman in Beckford Churchyard, at the foot of Bredon Hill, in Worcestershire, dating from the same century as William James. "Sarah Dyer", I read, "died 1838. *She was a daily letter carrier*. And walked about 16 miles a day; in all, some 90 thousand miles!"

Among my friends, to this day, is a New Zealand postwoman who came regularly to our letter box at the bottom of the road, when we lived at "West Hills". (She is now married, with a family, but I meet her occasionally; and she phones me from time to time. We both belong to the one *worldwide* Methodist Church!) I must think to ask her if she knows that the *first* Wesleyan wife in this country was "Catherine", wife of the Church's *first* missionary, the Reverend Samuel Leigh. After they arrived, in a fragile sailing ship from England, she waited *nine*

Sharing Surprises

teen months to receive her first letter from home! (And the news would be old, when she did get it!) It stands indicative of pioneer courage, and loneliness, in that same century of William James and Sarah Dyer, the eighteen-hundreds!

Things are, of course, very different now, for letter writers, carriers and receivers, though "zest" is as important as ever, in our air mailed, sharing lives! Mails between here and "the old country", as the birthplace of countless settlers, who came later than the Leighs, were exceedingly precious!

One dear English friend of mine, the wife of a doctor, who came out with him to our country by way of a part-life-time of service on a Leprosy Island in the Pacific (which I've had the "pleasure" of visiting), is still one of my most "zestful" letter writers and receivers. A widow now, and aged, she lately surprised me greatly by sending me back, for re-reading and any use I might be able to make of them, *all the letters I had written to her – seventy-two of them*! Neatly packed, each with a brief written hint of its content, they covered many "ups-and-downs" of life, and distant travels, I found, when I settled happily to going through them again. My ever-handy dictionary defines *"zest"* as "invigorating or keen excitement, or enjoyment for living".

And I thank God for it!

As the Years Pass

Working and Wondering

Gracious God, forgive me that ever I forget that people matter more in this world, than anything else;

Forgive me that I make excuses for my carelessness – letting slip, again and again, chances to help and encourage others;

Save me from setting my eyes on distant places – overlooking chances of offering service near at hand!

Give me a strong rule, with regard to pride – let the loving spirit of Christ permeate all my thoughts and actions. I pray in His Name. Amen.

R.F.S.

We all need to find God – and He cannot be found in noise and restlessness. God is the Friend of silence.

See how Nature – trees, flowers, grass – grows in silence – the more we receive in silent prayer, the more we can give.

The essential thing is not what we say – but what God says to us.

Mother Teresa

Lord of our ongoing daily lives, we give thanks for good letters, as they come – and for every other helpful link in our lives.

R.F.S.

Sharing Surprises

I find Thy guidance, as I pause to reflect on good Jerome's words, as he wrote:

> I have had to give up writing the commentary on Ezekiel ... the crowds of homeless made me want to turn the words of Scripture into deeds, *not only saying holy things, but doing them*!

Gracious Lord, I am glad to be alive – and here!
Quicken my awareness of Thy daily presence.
All my days have added up to a growing-learning experience.
And I thank Thee for that – so helpful, so rich!
Never move from my side, I beseech Thee!

R.F.S.

Taking Levels

During my early twenties – some time ago now – it was my joy to be a student in my country's southern city of Christchurch. "The City of the Plains", as she was known near and far, moved one of our poets to thankfulness that "each of her streets was closed with shining Alps, like Heaven at the end of long plain lives". Among her other charms she had – and still has – her leisurely river, overhung with graceful willows, adding coolness, and banks grassed to the water's edge. Her beautiful gardens and tree-bordered squares – bearing the names of English martyrs: Latimer, Ridley, Cranmer – introduced a strong sense of history of the land of their birth that many were pleased to remember. Even more striking was her cathedral, with its tall spire, set in her central square. Raised by the pioneers in hard days, one would be dull, who overlooked its significance.

But some still do not know that they can step inside, and come upon a surprise inscription, which reads: "*On the floor below this wall is the benchmark, twenty feet above mean-level at Lyttelton* [the port, a goodly distance off] *from which all other levels in Christchurch are calculated.*" So that a surveyor or builder, set to raise a block of offices in the city, or a school, a hospital, or an aerodrome in the suburbs, must rightly take his levels from within the cathedral. And what a significant thing that is! *Things sacred are here*

Sharing Surprises

seen to affect things secular; and what is found established in the House of God, to govern men and women in their business and home life.

It doesn't take long for the wise and sensible amongst us to learn that there are a great many things in our human life that don't work out, until *we take our "levels" from the place of the Spirit!*

In 1937, I was present in London at the coronation of our present Queen's beloved father and mother, George VI and Queen Elizabeth, and I was moved to learn of an action of His Majesty, the very night before that great event. The Dean of Westminster received a telephone call: "I wish to come into the Abbey tonight." "Certainly, Sir," came the reply, "I will be there to receive you." "No, don't do that," the King answered, "I want you to see that the postern door is left open. I wish to come into the Abbey, and I wish to be alone."

And that night, the man who on the morrow – at short notice, as such great issues normally go – would himself be immersed in "pomp and circumstance" and leadership that would benefit his people, wanted, alone and on his knees before God, to *"check his levels"*!

He was familiar, of course, with the words of the Psalmist of long ago, who found himself faced with a situation he wasn't sure he could handle. (Psalm 73: 16-17; R.S.V.):

When I thought how to understand this, it seemed to me a wearisome task, until I went into the sanctuary of God, then I perceived their end.

And surely the secret of a Psalmist, and of a King, is secret enough for you and me!

Taking Levels

Working and Wondering

Every now and again, it is good to have a chance to "check one's levels". There are many ways in which it can be done – in silence; in a walk alone; in talk with a very close, trusted friend; in a word with one's minister; in prayer; in sharing in the Communion Service; in taking time to ponder the most searching parts of a devotional book one trusts.

Some while ago, I spent a whole day with the young pastor of "The Church of the Holy Carpenter", in Hong Kong. It was the only free day I had in that city. I prayed before the ordinary carpenter's bench, which is the altar there.

Here was no wedge driven between work and worship – as, surely, it never should be! It was good to ponder there *the worth of my work daily*, as my Master could do, in Nazareth. A carpenter's bench is always a symbol of ministry. What does it say to me about the work that I offer God?

The old philosopher of the Book of Ecclesiastes asks:

> You spend your life working ... and *what do you have to show for it*? ...
> The sun still rises, and it still goes down, going wearily back to where it must start all over again.
> The wind blows south, the wind blows north

Sharing Surprises

– round and round and back again.
Every river flows into the sea, but the sea is not yet full . . .

(Ecclesiastes 1:3-7; G.N.B.)

Don't you suppose that the Carpenter of Nazareth would have taken *His levels* before God?
And are we who follow Him not close enough to do the same?

Professor Murdock, of Melbourne, once wrote: "It is my faith that we are moving toward the day when all the hateful work in the world will be done by machines, and everyone will enjoy work."
But need we wait for that day – if it ever comes?

I feel that Jesus enjoyed His work in Nazareth. I can't forget that He said: "My Father worketh hitherto, and I work." (John 5:17; A.V.)

> All-loving – but Thy love is stern
>   And claims, not love alone, but deeds:
> It profits little if I burn
>   With rapture, while my brother bleeds;
> Further my love with practical intent,
>   Lest it evaporate in sentiment.

Anon

Easter Memories

High among the rewards of travel are *the surprises of recognition*. I have found it so again and again, and just now I'm thinking of my stay in old Jerusalem.

From my simple lodging – St George's Hospice, in the kindly shadow of its cathedral – I walked a short distance to where the Nablus Road merges with the wide pavement before the Damascus Gate. There is no missing that – its tall ramparts beneath the blue sky, hot sunshine on its ancient stone. Bible figures there go about their business, each man in his long garment of striped cotton under a top wool cloak, which he would fling off indoors.

Near the entrance, a squatting salesman constantly tended a little pile of beans heaped on the pavement, his bobbing head in a red fez prepared for the hot sun. Others walked gracefully, each with a white *kaffiŷeh* flowing from the head, with rings of black goat-hair keeping it in place. (I had to pinch myself to recognize these as real people, and not colour pictures of a Bible story book.)

At that early hour only a few women were hastening to and fro, there, to make good the needs of their families in the adjacent market. But there was no missing their attractive garments, in hand-worked reds, terracottas and greens. I understood that morning what Renan meant last century, when he said: *"The Holy Land is the Fifth Gospel."* Matthew,

Sharing Surprises

Mark, Luke, John and this – and ever so much more like it!

Supported in the same living dimension, hours later, I made my way towards the holy Garden of Gethsemane, its solitary vine near the entrance offering a widely-open passion-flower, with a cross at its heart. And beyond the gate, as I pushed it open, a glimpse of the Garden's gnarled olive trees, blue-green. A gentle old Brother, sandal-footed and carrying a hoe, moved forward in his rusty-dun habit to help me. Among those eight historic trees – saplings that had carried life forward from those of Bible times – was the same historic quietness!

In another part of the city next day, a gentle Sister of another Order received me below ground level, at a historic spot beneath great buildings, on the site of our Lord's Judgement. Removing a piece of cloth covering, she drew my attention to a deeply scratched version of the game "Noughts and Crosses", that the Roman soldiers played there, when time hung heavy as they waited for judgements to conclude. And in that reduced light, as I looked upon it in the Fortress of Antonia, Scripture came alive. Then we moved in the direction of a deep, dark cistern at our feet. Was it from this – still, now, as then, full of water – that Pilate drew what he needed on the world's greatest Judgement Hour, to wash his hands, as a wicked gesture of irresponsibility. Almost certainly.

Then that Friday afternoon, by invitation, I walked, slowly and quietly, with a little company of silent, reverent Franciscans, along the Way of the Cross, the *Via Dolorosa*, pausing at intervals for silent prayer.

Working and Wondering

Countless times, these words have come back to my mind, words that my friend, the Rev. James Asa Johnson, sent to me when first he wrote them:

> It was a man like me
> who kissed the Master in the Garden,
> A man like me who bound His hands
> and led Him into Pilate's Hall.
> A man like me who shouted, "Crucify!"
> Who washed his hands,
> Who jeered and mocked . . .
> It was a man like me who drove the nails,
> whose spear was thrust into His side.
> It was a man like me who said, "Come down,
> And then we will believe!"
> *It was a man like me – so like*
> *I dare not look again*
> *for fear that it was I!*

Yes, Renan was right about "the Fifth Gospel"! So many words can now walk up and down in my mind and heart with new meaning!

Sharing Surprises

Central – on that "Hill of Crosses Three", He died –

> And sitting down, they watched Him there,
> The soldiers did;
> There, while they played with dice.
> He made His sacrifice,
> And died upon the Cross to rid
> God's world of sin . . .
> And ere His agony was done,
> Before the westering sun went down,
> Crowning that day with its crimson crown,
> He knew that He had won!
>
> Padre G.A. Studdert-Kennedy

Our wayside planet, carrying land and wave,
Love and life multiplied, and pain and bliss,
Bears as chief treasure, one forsaken grave.

Alice Meynell

On the Lake's Rim

A lovely day, the morning promised, the sky blue and high overhead. I would be busy later on. But just now, I had a little leisure – and where could I better spend it?

I was at the heart of New Zealand's thermal activity, known the world round; though not all who knew about it had found their way to St Faith's Maori church, with its beautiful handwork within. Alone, at that early hour, I looked out through the recently added chapel window, depicting the manly figure of the Lord and Master, by Galilee. Stepping across the Lake, He was strikingly shown, coming towards one. It was proper that His manly-fitness should be shown by the wearing of a *korowai* about his shoulders – a chief's woven Maori cloak, with a fringe of native bird feathers. He was the strong, young Man of the carpenter's bench striding freely. There was nothing weakly effeminate about Him – as shown all too often in painters' representations offered to the world. How could there be? If he had been pasty-faced and flat-chested, He could not have done the work required at His bench in Nazareth, using saw, hammer and plane to fashion things to meet practical needs – plough-beams, and yokes, and household chests.

He is properly shown as a young Man, with a lightly-bearded chin, His eyes straight and kindly.

Sharing Surprises

The craftsman in glass has clearly desired that we should understand Him to be the strong, fit, young Man that Peter and the rest of those sturdy fisherman of Galilee knew Him to be.

His call to them was "*Follow Me!*" – *and they followed*! Being "fishers of men" was a task as demanding as anything they'd ever done! The beloved lake they knew best, with its mighty winds funnelling down from the hills, was not always calm – far from it! I'll never forget its many moods. But the record stands: "Straightway, they left their nets – and followed Him" (Matthew 4:18-20; A.V.).

In my growing up into discipleship, I was to read the telling comment of young Professor Herbert Butterfield of Cambridge University: "*Hold to Christ*, and for the rest be totally uncommitted!" And I've never moved past that reality. "Spirituality is at the heart of our efforts to be human. It is the reflection of our inner, honest, searching, hoping heart. It is the style of our judging and acting, and the quality of our loving. It is the voice of our prayer, and the progress of our pilgrimage."

I was persuaded of this afresh, when I stepped from St Faith's today, as aware as ever of my challenge to Christian discipleship. In the voice of the Living, Risen Christ, down the long shore of the years: – "*Follow Me!*"

On the Lake's Rim

Working and Wondering

Jesus calls us! O'er the tumult
   Of our life's wild restless sea,
Day by day His voice is sounding,
   Saying: "Christian, follow Me".

As of old, apostles heard it
   By the Galilean lake,
Turned from home and toil and kindred
   Leaving all for His dear sake.

Jesus calls us from the worship
   Of the vain world's golden store,
From each idol that would keep us,
   Saying: "Christian, love Me more".

Cecil Frances Alexander

Thou knowest, O Lord, the duties that lie before us this day; and the sins that so easily beset us.
Guide us, strengthen us, and protect us, O Lord, our Strength and our Redeemer. Amen.

Mabel Dearmer

Now unto Him that is able to keep you from falling, and to present you faultless before the presence of His glory with exceeding joy, to the only wise God our Saviour, be glory and majesty, dominion

Sharing Surprises

and power, both now and ever. Amen.

Jude verses 24 & 25; A.V.

Into Thy hands, O God, we commend ourselves this day; let Thy presence be with us to its close. Enable us to feel that in doing our work, we are doing Thy will; and that in serving others we are serving Thee; through Christ our Lord, Amen.

Uppingham School Prayer Book

I bless Thee, O Lord, for gifts of energy and thought, for friendliness, and love, for work to do, in this great world of endless fascination and challenge.

R.F.S.

Strengthen my will-power this day, O Lord, that I may praise Thee, and serve Thee. Amen.

R.F.S.

A Surprise One Season

Have you ever been a guest of the Queen, and walked in the garden of Buckingham Palace? I was surprised by the size of it, when once upon a time it was my pleasure to attend a Royal Garden Party.

I had been a number of weeks in England's southern Spring countryside, in perfect weather. Turning from Wells Cathedral, one mid-afternoon, I paused at a post office to collect accumulated mail, and on the top of it awaited my Royal Command. I opened it first – as was only fitting – the moment I could move off with my haversack, to a grassy spot under a shady hedge. London – with its call for a best frock, long gloves, and a shady hat – seemed an impossible distance away!

But, of course, I went, and so saw the Garden, later returning to Wells, with my haversack, to go on with my walk. But ever since, whenever I see any pictures or write-ups of happenings there, I prick up my interest. I did so a while ago, when I chanced to read that a party of twenty-six naturalists had moved in, at the Queen's gracious invitation, to count every living thing that grows, flies, creeps, or so much as crawls there! It surprised me that there were no squirrels – only lots of cheeky Hanoverian rats, and little shy mice. And nineteen kinds of birds – even very beautiful ones – mallard duck, wood-pigeon, pied wagtail and spotted flycatcher. One by one

Sharing Surprises

they were listed, not forgetting eighty-seven kinds of beetles – some very handsome. There were also fifty-seven kinds of spiders; thirteen caddis-flies, and over a hundred kinds of other flies and plant-bugs, plus *three* mosquitoes – which must have gladdened all concerned! And but *one* large water-flea, thought to have come in, perhaps, on the pink flamingoes, and *one* lone African moth!

A census we might call that count; though it was of course simpler than that which concerns us men and women, from time to time. People, of course, *have been counted more precious*, going right back to what has been called "the world's first census", at the birth of the Baby Jesus! Christmas by Christmas, we still remember it.

I've no idea how the Queen thinks of her garden-creatures, each endowed with a measure of simple life! Does she have favourites? But God thinks about each of us individually, and values us.

Human values are lastingly important to our Lord, wherever life may set each one of us down! "I see quite plainly *that God has no favourites*, but that he who reverences Him and lives a good life in any nation, is welcomed by Him" (Acts 10:34-35; Moffatt's Translation).

"Where, in heaven's name," asked the distinguished Christian world citizen of our day, Barbara Ward, "can we discover any limit to a Divine purpose that the wide bounty of the Universe has been designed chiefly to benefit twenty per cent of its inhabitants?"

A Surprise One Season

Working and Wondering

O Earth! thou hast not any wind that blows
Which is not music; every weed of thine
Pressed rightly flows in aromatic wine;
And every humble hedge-row flower that grows,
And every little brown bird that doth sing,
Hath something greater than itself, and bears
A living word to every living thing.
Albeit it holds the Message unawares.

Richard Realf

In the beginning God created the heaven and the earth. And the earth was without form, and void; and the darkness was upon the face of the deep. And the Spirit of God moved upon the face of the waters. And God said, Let there be light; and there was light. And God saw the light, that it was good; and God divided the light from the darkness ... And God called the dry land Earth, and the gathering together of the waters called he Seas: and God saw that it was good ... And God said, Let the waters bring forth abundantly the moving creature that hath life, and fowl that may fly above the earth in the firmament of heaven ... And God said, Let the earth bring forth the living *creature after his kind ... and creeping thing* ... And God saw that it was good. And God said, Let us make man in our image ...

Book of Genesis

Sharing Surprises

> All things bright and beautiful,
>   All creatures great and small,
> All things wise and wonderful,
>   The Lord God made them all.
>
> Cecil Frances Alexander

Perhaps this is the right moment to remember that it isn't enough to teach our children to sing these words – as long as life lasts we have a duty together, holidays and all, to tend His living creatures – *some of which are our pets.*

> Cuckoo, cuckoo, cuckoo!
> Above the thrush and linnet,
> Above the shrilling lark,
> He shouted to the morn,
> As if the Earth were born
> That very April minute,
> And he the first bird in it!
>
> By my late loved friend, Teresa Hooley,
who cherished all creatures

His Footprints

Seven minutes from home, at seven o'clock this Summer morning, I set off to the beach, and was surprised to see that I was not the first – there were footprints! I stooped to examine them. Then, as I continued, Mr Standfast's lovely words came to my mind with a fresh challenge. "I have loved to hear my Lord spoken of," said he, "and wherever *I have seen the print of His shoe in the earth*, there I have coveted to set my foot, too." Lovely words to walk up and down in the mind of any one of us!

It was easy there, in the freshness of that morning, to rejoice in the very many places where I had seen them, as I had gone about the world, whenever men and women had set *forgiveness* and *peace* in the place of anger and revenge; where many a one had set beauty in the place of ugliness in human relationships; where large generosity had been set to take a place of hurt; and good faith been established in the place of distrust.

J.R. Miller, who had observed this spirit of the Master's "Good Samaritan" upon the merciless Way, rejoiced to say: "The best evidence of the divinity of Christ is not in any number of proof-texts gathered from all parts of the Bible, and arranged in order, *but in the works that Christ has done, and is doing every day!*" They are seldom reported in the headlines and prominent places in our newspapers – but those who have

Sharing Surprises

eyes to see do not doubt that "some Good Samaritan" has been at work there in Christ's Spirit. Since "The Road from Jerusalem to Jericho" runs through every crisis area of this modern world – and *"Christ's footprints" are to be seen there*!

It is a sun-baked road (as many a missionary doctor, many a nurse, many a lay-worker, and priest can report)

> *But some who walk it find*
> *The footprints of a Traveller,*
> *With Love upon His mind.*

It is the discovery of many of us – in modern homes for lepers; in Blind Institutes for needy ones bereft of sight; and in classes for the denied deaf. Again and again, in distant countries to which I have travelled, I have rejoiced in such a find! And He is not to be missed in gracious, clean, happy homes provided for little needy children. I have been in many! And in homes, the world round, provided for the lonely and frail aged, needing peaceful, understanding support, at life's end.

Says Dr Paul Tournier, the distinguished Christian psychiatrist, "The adventure of Faith is exciting, difficult and exacting, but full of poetry, of new discoveries, *of fresh turns and sudden surprises*!"

His Footsteps

Working and Wondering

We have been promised a safe arrival but not a smooth voyage.

Henry Dubanville

But we know that Christ is at hand to support us, through His compassionate disciples of this day. "*The power of Love* is that which seizes the emotive springs of a person, so that he really feels the matter deeply . . . because *without action* he wouldn't be comfortable. *So it's not* merely a *feeling*, and it's not merely a *doing*. It's both!"

James Dunn, Professor of Divinity at the University of Durham. (He teaches New Testament and the Origins of Christianity, and is a Methodist local preacher.)

The story of the Good Samaritan is in The New Testament, Luke 10:29-37. *In a quiet moment, re-read this, as if you had never read it before*!

And may Christ deliver you from excuses. Says one in our needy world:

> Don't ask us to feed the multitudes;
> Our hands might suddenly
> Smell of fish,
> And crumbs could catch
> In our trouser-cuffs.

Anon

Sharing Surprises

Aware of Christ, our modern day poet, Thomas Curtis Clark, whom I met, wrote very tellingly:

> I saw Him once – He stood a moment there;
> He spoke one word, which laid my spirit bare;
> He grasped my hand, then passed beyond my ken;
> *But what I was, I shall not be again.*

In a quiet moment of reflection, teach me, O Lord, the deep meaning of a simple prayer:

> Lord, make old people tolerant,
> Young folk sympathetic,
> Great folk humble,
> Busy folk patient,
> Bad folk good,
> *And make me what I ought to be.* Amen.

Anon

Personal and Precious

I hope your letter box brings you *welcome surprises* from time to time – mine does! It's not often that I seek permission to share in a book such as this, what comes in that way. Some of my mail from far places, I confess, I do keep by me to read and re-read. Yet there are times when I'm near to being overwhelmed by that loved letter box. These days, too much of too little worth finds its way there – a cluster of bright leaflets from a Food-Market; a delicate communication from a recently opened jeweller's in the next town; two sample magazines of the smart sexy sort I never read; and a roughly handwritten note from some eager fellow ready to mow my lawns, or top my trees. By the weekend there is quite an accumulation.

Mercifully, this varying lot doesn't have to be carefully read, or even kept, or I'd soon be on the street. There is no average flat that could deal with it all! But *real* mail I must have, dealing with the issues I care about. They help to nourish the spirit! And occasionally, there's one so "Personal and Precious" that only when I've memorized it do I take it away to a safe place, where I tuck it within a rubber band.

The first I kept – following on talk with an aged, widely revered scholar, a few days earlier, began "Dear Rita, I am a little shy about a letter after our talk – but I feel I want to send you one. (If you should use

Sharing Surprises

it ever, please do not so much as hint at the identity of your sender.)" And he went on, to get to the heart of his one-time hard working Yorkshire family, who never once, over the years, chanced to see this little land of his adoption and life-service.

"My father," he began, "was the talkative one; Mother under much better control, where words were in question. *But how she loved us!*

"Just before I set off to join my ship when the time came to sail to New Zealand," he added, "my father said much; but Mother very little. I slept in the attic that last night – but I couldn't sleep.

"It must have been nearly midnight," he went on, "when I heard footsteps coming up the stairs. Mother came into my room, carrying a lighted candle. I pretended to be asleep, as best I could. She held her light above my head, then sat down on the chair beside my bed. (I peeped, and saw that she was crying softly.) Then with her other hand, she touched my hair – so gently, over and over, as if to keep the likeness imprinted there for ever.

"After what seemed to me a long time, she slowly moved from the chair, and made to go – she did not speak. And it's now well over fifty years", he added. "The wonder is, *Love can always find its own surprising way of speaking!*"

Working and Wondering

Eternal Father, Lord of Life, and lasting Love, I open my eyes to the light of this new day, with wonder.

My heart borrows words from the long ago: *"This is the day which the Lord hath made: I will rejoice, and be glad in it"* (Psalm 118:24; A.V.).

Another's words strengthen me as I set about offering service today: *"The Lord hath appeared of old unto me, saying, 'Yea, I have loved thee with an everlasting love'"* (Jeremiah 31:3; A.V.).

He that dwelleth in love dwelleth in God, and God in him (1 John 4:16; A.V.).

> O Love that wilt not let me go,
> I rest my weary soul in Thee:
> I give Thee back the life I owe,
> That in Thine ocean depths its flow
> May richer, fuller be.
>
> George Matheson

I may speak with the tongues of men and of angels
    but if I have no love, I am a noisy gong or a
    clanging cymbal;
I may prophesy, fathom all mysteries and secret lore,
I may have such absolute faith that I can move
    hills from their place, but if I have no love,
    I count for nothing;

Sharing Surprises

I may distribute all I possess in charity,
I may give up my body to be burnt,
    but if I have no love,
    I make nothing of it.

1 Corinthians 13:1; Moffatt

    Love ever gives –
        Forgives – outlives –
    And ever stands
        With open hands.
    And while it lives,
        It gives,
    For this is Love's prerogative –
        To give – and give – and give.

Unknown

God's Point of View

I was staying in Boston, guest in a gracious family home, going back six generations. And whilst there, an admirer of that unusual American character, Henry David Thoreau, called round in her car. We talked of the little I knew of him, and his nature-loving life and writings. And she offered to take me, that very morning, to some of his haunts. It was no great distance to Walden Pond, that he has made attractive the world over.

"I went to the woods", he was remembered as saying, "because I wished to live deliberately, to front only the essential facts of life, and see if I could learn what it had to teach, and not, when I come to die, discover I had not lived."

So there was something very purposeful about his modest retreat at Walden Pond, though he was no Robinson Crusoe. His little cabin was only a mile and a half from the centre of the village, and half a mile from the main road leading that way. He had callers, and took walks, sometimes daily into Concord. He was very eager to search out, in this and that, *a new point of view*.

That sounds well enough. But on one occasion, he went so far as to sink himself deeply in a marsh up to his neck, in order to get, he said, *"a frog's eye view of Nature"*.

Sharing Surprises

I'm wholly in favour of a fresh point of view from time to time, on most things, if we earth-humans are to grow in character and understanding. But I do draw the line at a day up to the neck in any marsh – and Thoreau did spend a whole day at it!

Phillips's modern New Testament translation gives a verse about a desire of St Paul's – it's in his letter to the Colossians (1:9). He says: "We are asking God that you may see things, as it were, *from His point of view*."

Have you ever thought that that was exactly what Jesus did when His disciples came saying that they had been refused accommodation in a certain Samaritan village, and suggesting that their Lord should "command fire to come down from heaven, and consume them" – and He turned and rebuked them (Luke 9:52-56). It was as if He was saying: "*That's not God's point of view!*"

Jesus spent all His ongoing Earth-life – in thought, prayer and practice towards the Kingdom – *interpreting God's point of view*! And that is His challenge that now comes to us, as His followers, in affairs of the Kingdom.

Einstein, one of our great scientific leaders in modern times, went so far as to say: "I try to consider the atom as God sees it." And one is bound to declare that if all nations, here and now, could do exactly that, it would rid us of our terrors. God must have a plan for the atom – He made it. *If only we could see it from "His point of view"!*

Easter Memories

Working and Wondering

Faithfully He deals and justly, trustworthy
  are all His precepts;
His orders are enacted for all time,
  issued in faithfulness and justice;
He has sent His people freedom,
  fixing His compact with them for all time –
A God majestic, terrible.
The first thing in knowledge is reverence
  for the Eternal.

Psalm 111:7-10; Moffatt

PRAYER
Gracious God my Eternal Father, on this given morning, as I waken, I praise Thee for the wonders of this world that Thou hast created.

Every tiny green shoot, every up-reaching tree, every living thing makes its natural response. But here and now, my human response must be much more meaningful.

Thou hast given me powers of body, mind and spirit – a unique capacity to worship Thee and work with Thee, in this great world. Enable me to offer love and faithfulness. Amen.

R.F.S.

Sharing Surprises

Quiet now,
Close the mind's door
On business of the day,
And for this brief moment
Clear the way
For God.

Helen Couch, *Rehabilitation*

I may speak with the tongues of men and of angels, but if I have no Love, I am a noisy gong or a clanging cymbal.

1 Corinthians 13

Eye hath not seen, nor ear heard,
neither hath entered into the heart of man,
the things which God hath prepared for them
that love Him.

1 Corinthians 2:9

Beauty We Must Have

Charles Kingsley is remembered to have exclaimed with surprise, on one unforgettable occasion: "*How beautiful God is! How beautiful God is!*"

But it's happened to me, again and again, and to lots of others of us – including yourself, maybe. It must have been an experience of this kind that long ago led the Psalmist to exclaim: "Let the beauty of the Lord our God be upon us: and establish Thou the work of our hands upon us" (Psalm 90:17; A.V.).

We see His beauty everywhere – sometimes magnificently stated, so that we are bound to exclaim! We can't help it. One walks on Exmoor, as I have done at *sundown* or from home, on this side of the world, climbed "One Tree Hill" with a friend, at *sunrise*, to welcome in a birthday!

And God shows Himself, too, of course, in less dramatic Beauty: the gentle skin-pink of a baby's face; the might and majesty of mountains; the colour of many a common flower, designed to attract passing bees, and thus secure fertilization. It just happens, you add, to be a biological necessity! But that, I believe, has been an over-stated theory right from the start. It doesn't account for forms of beauty that are unseen at the bottom of the sightless, lightless ocean; or, at a lesser depth, at many a lake-bottom – where are minute creatures so beautiful

Sharing Surprises

that, microscopically examined, they can be compared with the beauty of a rose-window in a gothic cathedral! Biological necessity – which sounds, in some situations, so very plausible – has nothing to say in others. It can't even explain the beauty of clouds at sunrise, or, for those who never rise early enough to see them, at sunset!

We are, in all honesty, left asking: "*Why* are so many things in Nature so beautiful?" The only answer that I've come upon, with anything to say to me about the presence of so much beauty in the world of Nature, is that God is a God of Beauty – *because He is a God of Love*! (I am almost driven to say: "He can't help it!") I have seen so many young mothers, stitching away at little garments for a coming child, in the happy ending of their nine months of womanly patience! Stitching a rose-bud here; a tiny spray there. Will her child sleep more blessedly, because of them? Not at all! But she can't help it – *because she is a lover*!

It is of the nature of a lover, to make something beautiful! And *God*, our Faith and Teaching tell us, *is Earth's Supreme Lover*! A line in the biblical Book of Wisdom has a point right here; it says: "Never wouldst Thou have created anything, *if Thou hadst hated it*!" Hate does not *create*, it destroys! Wherever I find beauty in the world I think of God! I know He has been about His best-loved "business" there. And I hum one of the two verses of the shortest hymn I know:

Beauty We Must Have

This, this is the God we adore,
Our Faithful unchangeable Friend;
Whose Love is as great as His power,
And never knows measure nor end!

Working and Wondering

God's Beauty on Earth comes in simple things,
as in great. Season by season brings
Assurance to our lives, of Lasting Love!

R.F.S.

It comes as one of many gifts –
  Forgiveness, Hope, Faith and Courage!
All essential to our earthly pilgrimage –
  and unfailingly bestowed!

Gracious God, accept my thanks
  for Thy creative Gifts –
And in Thy mercy, save me ever from casualness.
For Christ's sake. Amen.

R.F.S.

In the *Methodist Hymn Book* is a hymn by Benjamin Waugh, of which it is my pleasure to share three verses. It may be in your denominational Hymnal, and already loved by you.

Sharing Surprises

Now let us see Thy Beauty, Lord,
    As we have seen before;
And by Thy Beauty quicken us
    To love Thee and adore.

'Tis easy when with simple mind
    Thy loveliness we see,
To consecrate ourselves afresh
    To duty and to Thee.

Our every feverish mood is cooled,
    And gone is every load,
When we can lose the love of self,
    And find the Love of God.

PRAISE

Gracious God, we bless Thee, for every good gift in our lives. For everything of Beauty in our discipleship.

We thank Thee for the mountains, and grass and gardens that minister to our home-setting.

And for seas, and lakes; and rivers winding afar, we bring Thee thanks at holiday times.

Go with us, O God – among strangers, and friends, and bring us home, strengthened in body, and spirit;

    readytoserveTheeanew.InChrist'sName.Amen.

R.F.S.

A Woman of Words

I was surprised today, before rising to speak to a group at a luncheon, to be introduced as "A Woman of words"! Whether the bright chairman felt it was a compliment or not, I am at a loss to know, but smiles crossed the faces of many in that mixed audience. (Perhaps they thought it was inevitable!)

As far as I was concerned, I first loved words in childhood. When playing with a little friend, in the tall Summer grasses during holiday times, we could think of nothing better than, each day, choosing a fresh favourite word. And I can still remember some of them, all these years later: *Skipping, Laughter, Sparkle!*

And it's true, I've spent most of my grown up years since in sharing *spoken words* – in numerous pulpits and platforms the world round – and *written words* through books that have gone as far. And I still start out often on an exciting piece of sharing.

* * *

The beloved Authorized Version of the Bible has, of course, long been spoken of reverently as "The Word of God". And I can't think of anything amiss in that. It says so much! And to those of us who constantly read the Bible in the beautiful Authorized Version – the one that we first learned to read, and still rejoice

Sharing Surprises

in, along with the many modern versions — it *lives*!

I'm always finding something new among its long words and its short words — something lastingly true, something challenging and close to life. One of its very shortest words — of but two letters — the little word *do*, is all of that! And one finds it in both Old and New Testaments, indeed in the very first book of all, Genesis (31:16; A.V.): "Whatsoever God hath said unto thee, *do*." It's not a word that will ever go out of date, a word just to read, to listen to, and discuss, to argue about wordily. It's a little word that is sometimes uncomfortable — but we know, all too well, what it means. It's *a word of action with a lasting place in religion*.

The Psalmist uses it again, and again, beginning with that beautiful saying (Psalm 40:8): "I delight to *do* Thy will, O my God; yea, Thy Law *is within my heart*." It was not something that came to mind, for him, only once a week — as, alas, it does for some of us in these modern times.

For the Psalmist, and for many others following him, on through the centuries, that little live *do* had constant meaning. In Ecclesiastes 9:10 the same little word is on the lips of another unknown character, who pauses to say: "Whatsoever thy hand findeth to do, *do* it with all thy might." And when we come to the New Testament, it is one of the most meaningful words!

An early test that Jesus the Master addressed to His disciples comes down to us, translated into a directness that no modern Christian has reason to miss, in Matthew 5:47: "What *do* ye more than others?"

A Woman of Words

Working and Wondering

PRAYER

Let the sacredness of human life, and service, come home to me afresh this day, O Lord.

I would dedicate my faculties anew, in service. Let me this day do my ordinary work honestly and humbly.

I need constantly a true perspective – living patience, and Love.

And save me from moving through the day too seriously – set some laughter and song upon my lips.

Gracious Father, bless this day all who labour to lighten the lot of others. Amen.

R.S.F.

> What profit should we win the race
> To solve the mysteries of space
> To signal through ten thousand nights,
> If we neglect to read the Star
> Shining forever from afar,
> Of Jesus - cradled from His birth
> On the dark bosom of the earth?
> *And what are victories of skill*
> *Unless exploring in God's will,*
> *We prove the Love we here have found*
> In this our world – our holy ground?
>
> Catherine Baird

Sharing Surprises

"If one had never seen a hand," are the arresting words of Christopher Fry, our modern dramatist, "and were suddenly presented for the first time with this strange and wonderful thing, what a miracle . . . it would be!"

> The simple bending of my wrist,
> The dainty touch of finger-tip,
> The steel intensity of grip;
> A tool of exquisite design,
> With pride I think, *"It's mine! It's mine!"*
>
> Anon

(But here and now – as a modern disciple – surely I ought to think, *"It's His!"*)

A Well-Earned Name

Very few of us stay in one place all our working lives – that would be called unadventurous, dull. Even a devoted minister gets a move from parish to parish, from circuit to circuit if he's a Methodist.

John Wesley, in early times, was constantly moving, riding his horse around England. And when, in time, England sent Methodist preachers to young America, they were known as "circuit riders". It was an honourable name; but things have changed, save that the historic name "circuit" lives on for Methodist ministers, as it does for judges in England concerned for the administration of English justice. Again, it was an honourable name. I mention this as background, in telling of a good friend, the Rev. Charles Gallachar, in whose Australian home and circuit I once did some service. One evening, speaking of his several circuits, he said: "When a man begins, he gets what we call 'a good kick-off'. And at the end of his time, he gets 'a good kick-out' – but what he lives to need most is *'a kick in the interim'*."

A few years on, answering a ring at his front door one evening, he was *greatly surprised* to find a cheerful bunch of young people of the Church bearing smilingly a gift of books, and a generous supper! "What is this?", he asked, with raised eyebrows.

Sharing Surprises

"This," they joined in answer, "*is a kick in the interim!*"

Of course, there are endless ways in which encouragement can be spelled out in this world – but I liked this one! Original, too! One of the early surprises I came upon in my Bible reading was a verse in 1 Samuel 30:6 which says, "*David encouraged himself* in the Lord his God!" It wasn't at first clear to me how that could be – but I soon worked it out! And that made me ready for a passage in the *Life of Lord Grey* that I came upon, where his friend said: "I was feeling depressed this morning, so I went to see Grey. I wanted to be made to feel two inches taller!" Isn't that a need we all know at times? That was why many a hard-pressed student at Wellesley College found her way to the door of Alice Freeman Palmer, the beloved Principal. One of her strugglers said: "When I saw her, I felt I could do things I never dreamed of before . . . Whenever I think of her, I have a new sense of dignity in my life."

It might be the encouragement of a letter, at a "low" time. The secret stands revealed, at the end of one of St Peter's. Have you noticed it, I wonder? "I have written you *these few lines of encouragement* . . ." (1 Peter 5:12; Moffatt).

One of Paul's friends in ministry in the great world was Joseph, in time called Barnabas (Acts 4:36; Moffatt): "*Barnabas, Son of Encouragement!*"

Wouldn't it be wonderful to earn a nickname like that?

It would certainly be worth "a try"!

A Well-Earned Name

Working and Wondering

MORNING PRAYER

Gracious God, I do not take my good night's rest for granted. Nor do I forget the many not so blessed.

For a safe roof; for clean linen; a bedtime book; a light to read by, I give Thee thanks.

And for the new day that wakens me with a welcome, I bless Thee. Support me, in my going out today – and in my coming in.

Let the spirit of Jesus's Earth-ministry in little Nazareth – and ever wider and deeper – move me, I pray.

Strengthen my love for all with whom I have dealings. And let my home be a place of real fellowship, at day's end. Amen.

R.F.S.

EVENING PRAYER

Lord of Life, as the sounds of the day's busyness are hushed, I would bring Thee my praise and adoration.

As I settle to sleep, let me enjoy the peace of my home, and take time to reflect on the whereabouts of each person linked to this family.

Let us all know, in the deep places of the heart, joy and living Faith. Strengthen us in the values for which Christ lived – died – and rose again. Let us rejoice in His living presence, here and now. Amen.

R.F.S.

Sharing Surprises

Day by day, I rejoice in our rich inheritance.
   The heroes and the saints
     Thy messengers became;
   And all the lamps that guide the world,
     Were kindled at Thy Flame.

Percy Dearmer

PRAYER

O God of Life, and Service, I bless Thee for all who minister to young, and old, daily encouragement.
Sometimes, the going is hard, the way unsure, then we need kindly, wise support.
Sensitive to those about us, let us not be slow to offer what help we can.
   In the Name of Jesus Christ, our Lord. Amen.

R.F.S.

Wool-Gathering

I like the word – it has a nice leisurely Saturday sound! One who has spent childhood in a city might never have come upon it, but if, like myself, you have grown up in the living, wide, green countryside, it might have been one of your favourite words. Though it carried two meanings, of course, it might have been one of your favourite occupations for Saturday. Along the barbed-wire, and barberry divisions that kept sheep in where they were meant to graze, we children went with large paper bags, and gathered in the little "snags" of wool left behind. It was a pleasant task, and brought in a little pocket-money.

But life was not all Saturdays, of course, and there were other occasions at home, and school, when suddenly we were awkwardly challenged with, *"What! Wool-gathering again!"* It was then that our favourite Saturday word carried its second meaning, as given in the dictionary: "Idle, absent-minded indulgence in fantasy, day-dreaming."

This, we discovered later, was something that even adults knew something of, although there was no one to chide them. More than that – some were actually loved adults, even revered ministers.

One of them, of whom I first learned when I was almost grown up, was Dr George Morrison, minister of the well-known Wellington Church in Glasgow. (I

Sharing Surprises

knew him only through his books – I had one or two, and, as I was able, added to them. I'd just begun to read such books, really books of sermons, with stories popped in here and there.)

Little did I dream that a time would come, a long while on, when I would be guest-speaker from his pulpit, to a crowded company, with a "wired" overflow in an adjacent building. As I made my way up into that exalted place, where the good man had ministered, I recalled how I had read in one of his books – a confession of "wool-gathering"!

Surprising as it all was to me, I remembered early in his ministry his difficulty in controlling his vagrant mind, during private devotions. He tried, one way and another, to mend the matter, but it was not easy. Eventually, a moment came when he determined to handle the Lord's Prayer, for a start.

Never would he allow himself to rise from his knees until he had done more than merely *repeat* those lovely, Christly words that he'd grown up with, so that now they could glide over his speech without fully registering their content.

Ten times he made a deliberate effort to mend the matter – and *ten times* failed. Only at the eleventh time did he succeed in mastering his *"spiritual wool-gathering"*, to *pray* sincerely, meaningfully, the words of that prayer!

So it can be done – God be thanked – if "wool-gathering" is your hurdle, and mine, to overcome!

Wool-Gathering

Working and Wondering

The psalmist sounds to be a person very close to life, when he says:

> By God's help I shall maintain my cause;
> in God I trust without a fear . . .
> *I am under vows to Thee, O God:*
> *I will pay Thee my offering of praise,*
> for Thou hast saved my life from death,
> my feet from stumbling,
> that I might live, ever mindful . . . in the sunshine of life.
>
> Psalm 56:10-13; Moffatt

THE GENERAL THANKSGIVING
Almighty God, Father of all mercies, we Thine unworthy servants do give Thee most humble and hearty thanks for all Thy goodness and lovingkindness to us and to all men. We bless Thee for our creation, preservation, and all the blessings of this life; but above all for Thine inestimable love in the redemption of the world by our Lord Jesus Christ; for the means of grace and for the hope of glory. And we beseech Thee, give us that due sense of all Thy mercies, that our hearts may be unfeignedly thankful, and that we may show forth Thy praise, *not only with our words*, but in our lives; by giving up ourselves to

Sharing Surprises

Thy service, and by walking before Thee in holiness and righteousness all our days; through Jesus Christ our Lord, to whom with Thee and the Holy Ghost be all honour and glory, world without end. Amen.

Bishop Reynolds, 1599-1676

> O Eternal Light, shine into our hearts;
> Eternal Goodness, deliver us from evil;
> Eternal Power, be Thou our support;
> Eternal Wisdom, scatter our ignorance;
> Eternal Pity, have mercy on us.

Grant that with all our heart, and mind, and strength, we may evermore seek Thy face; and finally bring us by Thine infinite mercy, to Thy holy presence, through Jesus Christ our Lord.

Alcuin, A.D. 735-804

And a simple modern prayer:

> Loving Father, in Thy mercy, hold us in the hollow of Thy hand. Amen.

R.F.S.

Endless Caring

I was only one of countless readers cast down when Winifred Holtby died. I loved her books and articles, and found pleasure in the photograph of that handsome, tall, young Yorkshire woman. It seemed that by then she had reached her secret of speaking, and caring. And she was in a great many ways supported by her writing. Her books are still on many of our shelves.

After she had died, I met her long-time friend, Vera Brittain; and she seemed no stranger, either. Independently the two of us, to my surprise, were called to address a large rally in the Central Hall, London. When it was over, we were glad to share afternoon tea together, before we went our separate ways.

In a short while, Vera welcomed me to lunch at her home in Chelsea; and much later, when I was once again in London, to her flat in Westminster. By that time, we had exchanged books, and many letters, and had much to talk about. I especially appreciated her book *Testament of Friendship*, with its story of the years of close friendship with Winifred Holtby, and mutual travelling, studying, writing and speaking.

In one unforgettable passage she wrote of Winifred's living, loving, caring purpose:

I ask that I may be permitted to love much, to

Sharing Surprises

serve to the utmost of my capacity, to keep faith with that high vision which men call God. I shan't do it wholly, nobody does that; *I only want never to stop caring*. The other things don't matter.

This appeared early, in Winifred's eager youthful writing that many of us the world round came to know as *Letters to a Friend*.

And though, with the years, she matured, she never faltered in her deep-down desire to care. Thinking of her now, how well, it seems, her statement of desire could have a place in every devotional book of this nature. It has a New Testament ring about it. None of us can establish Christ's Kingdom values *without the capacity to care*.

No wonder Winifred was a sincere admirer of the saint of Assisi – Francis. And as I remember them both in this page – and their two centuries – they come to complement each other beautifully. Many in the world have long cherished *his* words: seeking to tie their lives to them:

> Lord, make me an instrument of Thy peace;
> Where there is hate, may I bring love;
> Where there is malice, may I bring pardon;
> Where there is discord, may I bring
>   harmony;
> Where there is error, may I bring truth;
> Where there is despair, may I bring hope;
> Where there is darkness, may I bring light;
> Where there is sadness, may I bring joy!

Endless Caring

Working and Wondering

MORNING PRAYER

O Lord of this shared life, I rejoice in dawn, that issues in this new day. The course of my "comings and goings" until sundown, and rest, and the kindly renewal of sleep.

I may meet fresh folk I have never met before, with new interests and concerns. Let me show respect, and every care in speaking, and *listening*. Save me from undue haste.

Above all, let me respond to "Thy still small voice" leading me in my choices. Guard me against selfishness and lofty pride, set some renewing laughter on my lips.

Let the sacredness of life come home again to me. Let me learn more of Thee from the love and kindly sharing of others. And hold us all in the hollow of Thy hand. Amen.

R.F.S.

EVENING PRAYER

I bless Thee, O Lord, for Thy gracious keeping, through all the dangers and false enticements of this day. Greater than Thy Majesty is Thy Joy; more lasting than all is Thy Mercy.

O God, give me a lively concern for all the lonely and the lost. Show me how I can be of strength to them in their concerns of the common day. Let my discipleship be real this day, in this place – and joyous. Amen.

R.F.S.

Sharing Surprises

For the benison of sunshine,
   and the beauty of rain;
For bird-song at morning,
   and star-shine at night;
For good and many-tasting food;
   for the great gift of sleep;
For the discoveries of science,
   and the heritage of art;
For the ministry of books;
   and for music beyond reach of words.
For the sanity of friendship;
   and the "madness" of love.
To our Lord, our God. Amen.

A.S.T. Fisher

Our Father, we have much to tell Thee –
   help us to speak;
Thou hast much to tell us –
   help us to listen!

Anon

O Lord, let *the supremacy of Thy Caring* hold us steady in all our "comings" and "goings", we earnestly, trustingly pray. Amen.

R.F.S.

Endless Caring

Heavenly Father, blot out, we beseech Thee, our past transgressions; forgive us all our negligences and ignorances, and lift us up to new energy of mind, and devotion of heart – through Jesus Christ our Lord.

from Rydal School Hymnal

Surprises at Work

It's still easier to be a success with things than with people – it's still easier to make a living than a good life, isn't it?

In the great Inter-Church Centre in New York is a wonderful sculptured mural, in the entrance. It shows – as representative of the wide range of possibilities today – a scientist in his laboratory, a labourer carrying a bag of cement, a housewife preparing a meal, a tailor cutting cloth, a teacher instructing her class, a typist at her office desk, a farmer gathering grain, a doctor caring for the sick, etc. Amid the company stands a minister of the Gospel; and summarizing the whole is the inscription: *"Whatever ye do, do all to the glory of God."*

To lay hold of this is to understand Vocation. The clear of mind and spirit, of course, have seen it from the start. It goes back to the Incarnation. Christianity nowhere draws a line between what is sacred and what is secular.

> Now is the holy not afar
>   In temples lighted by a star,
> Now that the King has gone this way,
>   *Great are the things of every day!*

There is no doubt about the *surprise* of those who found the young Messiah's life to be a whole – like the robe He wore, woven throughout without a seam.

Surprises at Work

Listening to His teaching, the question that rose most readily to their lips was, "Is not this the Carpenter?"

Jesus was not play-acting in Nazareth; He was earning a living, and serving the needs of the community. And so well did He do it, that when setting out on what some have called His "sacred" ministry – preaching, teaching, healing – He was able to begin where people knew Him. He ran no risk – there was nobody in that crowd who could interject: "Carpenter, the stool you made for me has a wobbly leg", or "The chest won't shut to keep out the moths", or "The ox-yoke you sold me is rough, and galls the poor beasts". No!

"And what was done in the Carpenter's shop", Evelyn Underhill reminds us, "can be done in the engineer's shop, too." The same glorious wholeness must characterize our work today. "No amount of worship", as one overseer in our setting puts it, "will compensate for functional inefficiency. The man, the woman we sign on is not a Christian worker by reason of church-going alone, but because he, and she, believes in God, in this world of God's, and does *everything* to the glory of God!" So one by one our prayer must be:

> Son of the carpenter, receive
>   This humble work of mine;
> Worth to my meanest labour give
>   By joining it to Thine!

Unknown

Sharing Surprises

Working and Wondering

Seven whole days, not one in seven,
  I will praise Thee!

> George Herbert, 1632

Work should be prayer, if all be wrought,
  As Thou wouldst have it done;
And prayer, by Thee inspired and taught,
  Itself *with work be one!*

> John Ellerton, 1893

A hymn for when work is over, is in *The Methodist Hymn Book* (No. 951)

> The toils of day are over;
>   We raise our hymns to Thee,
> And ask that free from peril
>   The hours of dark may be;
> O Jesu, keep us in Thy sight,
> And guard us through the coming
>   night.

> Anatolius, 8th or 9th century

There are types of work which must be done again and again. Some, we think of as commonplace. (But is any work that is done with the right spirit, commonplace?) There is, perhaps, some complaint

Surprises at Work

with the writer, who paused long enough to set down the words: "Ten thousand times I've done my best; *and all's to do again!*"

The old Greeks pictured their deities, as living in a distant Olympus, quaffing their nectar, pursuing their own pleasures, aloof, unconcerned about the affairs of men; but the words of Jesus were, "*My Father worketh hitherto and I work.*"

John 5:17; A.V.

A good question is: "*Why* is our work important? *Is it because our Lord wants it*? Or because He wants *us*?

I will never let myself forget that the disciples whom Jesus called were working men: Peter, a fisherman – with work that had to be done "again and again". And one called was a tax-gatherer – with a despised job!

R.F.S.

A Gift of Love

A surprise waited for me in Kyoto. I had only been a few days in Japan before reaching that great city. There, among the many buildings one could visit, was one with a hard-to-remember name: "Higashi-Honganji Temple". It was not ancient, as things are counted "ancient" thereabouts. I found it set behind a well-established wall, running beside a main street. It had trees, though not as many as some temples I'd already entered.

There are old people still living who remember when this Temple was built, but few now. And there is to be had – after much searching – a little book in English called *A Daughter of the Samurai*. It tells of an early happening, from the viewpoint of a little Japanese girl.

"One day," she says, "Ishi, my nurse, and I were standing within our great gateway, watching the people pass. I noticed that almost every woman had her head wrapped in the blue-and-white towel that servants wear when dusting, or working in the kitchen!"

Curious to know the reason, she there and then summoned up courage to ask. "Those women," replied Ishi, "have cut off their hair." But it was still quite a puzzle, till she was told more, since the custom was that only widows did that, burying half with their husbands, and keeping the other half till

A Gift of Love

they themselves died. But soon, she learned the real reason in this instance. All the women – for the love of their hearts – had cut off the beautiful hair that they valued so much, to put it together to make a great rope, stronger than any other, that could heave into place the heavy central beam of the Temple then being built. One young woman cut off so much hair that she had to wait a further three years for her marriage – no man would marry her "looking like a widow". It could only be counted a bad omen.

"Our family," said the writer of the little book, "did not belong to the Shin sect of Buddhists [the builders of the Temple] but every woman, of whatever sect, wanted to have a part in the holy cause. And her hair was given freely, to join with the love-donations others had given."

Now, rolled round and round into a mighty coil of rope, it is counted a precious thing, having done its duty – *every part of the two hundred and sixty nine feet of its length*!

* * *

To look upon it was a moving experience, even for a Christian. It sent one back to the New Testament story of a woman who spilled over the feet of Jesus, her Master, her box of sweet-refreshing ointment, then washing His feet with her tears, and wiping them with the hairs of her head ... "For He said to her, 'Go in peace!' " (Luke 7:37-50; A.V.) A great surprise – *it's a story that should remain forever un-forgotten.*

Sharing Surprises

Working and Wondering

The Kingdom of God is lastingly established in Love!
R.F.S.

And can Horatius Bonar's loved hymn ever become out of date?

> O Love of God, how strong and true;
>   Eternal, and yet ever new;
> Uncomprehended and unbought,
>   Beyond all knowledge and all thought!
>
> O, wide-embracing, wondrous Love;
>   We read Thee in the sky above,
> We read Thee in the earth below,
>   In seas that swell and streams that flow.
>
> We read Thee best in Him who came
>   To bear for us the Cross of shame,
> Sent by the Father from on high,
>   Our life to live, our death to die.

The wonder of the Incarnation we see in *Jesus Christ's earthly interpretation of Love*. Catching His spirit, one of His close friends wrote of it, that we, following on, might get our values right:

> Look, Father, look on His anointed face,
>   And only look on us, as found in Him;

A Gift of Love

Look not on our misusings of Thy grace,
  Our prayer so languid, and our faith so dim.
For lo! between our sins and their reward
  We set the Passion of Thy Son, our Lord!

William Bright

"Many years ago," said a widely travelled doctor, "I wandered into a little Breton cathedral, and found a side chapel, bare and empty. It had no altar, and no priest; but carved on a stone wall, hung a figure of the Crucified. And underneath was written: *C'est ainsi qu'il m'a aimé* – He loved me like this!"

Let us put our love not into words or into talk, but into deeds, *and make it real*.

1 John 3:18; Moffatt

Courage – and Compassion

Life is full of surprises, isn't it? Even in the middle of Winter, as we are now. Last month I had cramp in a leg, *that nobody knew about*. This month, "Tishoo! Excuse me!" I have a cold, *that everybody knows about*!

And that's how things have always been, it seems. Thousands of years back, we are told, the physician, Sckhetenanach, "cured Pharaoh's nose". And that so welcome feat has never been allowed to be overlooked. Carved in stone, among the shifting sands and glories of old Egypt, that some of us go from the ends of the earth to see, the record remains. Sckhetenanach did not affect the fortunes of the reigning household, nor hold back invading armies from the doors; but he did cure Pharaoh's nose! And at the moment, with my own cold, I'm in the mood to say, "Let the record of his important achievement stand, as designed, till the end of Time!"

As a youngster, loving books, I was given many, and for one birthday, one splendid *Book of Heroes*, by Arthur Mee, that I valued greatly. It was there that I first met Charles Lamb. *"By universal consent,"* said Mee, *"he was one of the most lovable characters, a truly heroic figure."* But not with a cold? No! Listen to this. Armed with an enormous handkerchief, his feet in a steaming foot-bath, he wrote:

Courage – and Compassion

Did you ever have a very bad cold? This has been for many weeks my lot, and my excuse! My fingers drag heavily over this paper, and to my thinking it is three-and-twenty furlongs from here to the end of this half-sheet. I have not a thing to say. [He pauses a moment to seek out his handkerchief, then continues.] Nothing is of more importance than another. I am flatter than a pancake, emptier than a judge's wig when his head is not in it, duller than a stage when the actors are off it. I inhale suffocation; nothing interests me. If you told me the world will be at an end tomorrow, I should say, "Will it?" I have not enough will to dot my i's. My hand writes, not I, from habit . . . Oh, for a vigorous fit of toothache – an earwig in the ear, a fly in the eye – but this apathy!

Exactly! And this is the fine figure in the *Book of Heroes*? Yes, but each great hour brings its own challenge. *It's not there that we fail – it's in the long-dragged-out misery of a dull and ordinary struggle.*

Of all the ills iniquitous,
The cold is most ubiquitous.
Throughout the whole community
No one has much immunity.
It comes to every national,
To sane, and to irrational,
To debtor and to creditor,
Illiterate and editor,
To wicked and to pious folk,
To open-minded and biased folk . . .

So, have courage – and show compassion!

Sharing Surprises

Working and Wondering

To eyes wide open, and spirits aware, this world is a wonderful place –

> Now is the holy not afar
>   In temples lighted by a star;
> Now that the King has gone this way,
>   Great are the things of every day.

What did Our Lord mean when He said of God, in this world, "My Father is working still, and I am working?" (John 5:17; R.V.S.). Certainly He was not thinking of "holy places", sermons; *nor* things remote from this earth-life. *He spoke of ordinary things, that could add something of beauty and worth to life.*

He spoke of yokes –

(Matthew 11:29,30)

He made them as a Carpenter:

He spoke of barns –

(Luke 12:16-21)

When He laid aside the chisel and the adze, and stepped down to the river to be baptized, God spake, saying: "Thou art My beloved Son; in thee I am well-pleased."

(Luke 3:23)

Courage – and Compassion

What had He done, to so please God? He had not yet moved beyond His home circle! Preached no sermons!

But *He had shared much of extraordinary worth, with ordinary people! And much beauty*! And widely shared "difficult political times"!

One, of times very like our own, said:

> The world stands out on every side
> No wider than the heart is wide;
> Above the world is stretched the sky,
> No higher than the soul is high!
>
> Edna St Vincent Millay

PRAISE
> So shall no part of day or night
>   From sacredness be free;
> But all my life, in every step
>   Be fellowship with Thee. Amen.
>
> Horatius Bonar

One Needs to Know

There are many areas of life where this is true, and one does not travel far without making that discovery.

As a writer, I am glad that my home is not far from my local library, which offers me help at many points, on top of the many books of reference my own study shelves afford.

Today, as I left the long-familiar pavement and went into the library for help, I happened upon two men in "earnest whispers", as befitted the scene. One was the Chief Librarian, still youngish, and the other a "silvery-headed" gentleman and, seemingly, a little deaf. As my need brought me to a section of the same shelf, I couldn't help hearing his one brief sentence, after a pause: "*I don't know!*"

Then with a reference book under his arm, that the Chief Librarian had evidently persuaded him to leaf through before I arrived on the scene, I purposely moved out of range of their conversation. So intent were they, they mightn't even have noticed me – *but I noticed them*! And I came home remembering those three words of their "troubled" conversation that I'd heard.

For it is a "trouble", *not to know what one needs to know*! It was this simple, everyday fact that struck me when first my friend Rene and I were in London together, and fortunate enough to take some

One Needs to Know

lectures under Sir Walford Davies, Master of the King's Music; Lecturer at Gresham College. One night there, before we went home, we met up with a musical friend of Rene's, a great admirer of Sir Walford. And he told us of one occasion, known to him, when a young student came to the master, shyly proffering his autograph-book. Sir Walford took it, saying simply: "I will write here for you the *two notes* with which Handel began his greatest solo in *Messiah*, '*I know* that my Redeemer liveth!' " (And he set down the lines, treble clef, and two notes, saying as he did so, " '*I know!*' has long been my inspiration.")

Though many of us hear *Messiah* once a year at least, we need to be reminded of the importance of these two simple words! Without such, any Christian in our midst lacks a religious essential! We may know ourselves that when the words were first coined, they carried an Old Testament content, borrowed from one man's deep experience (Job 19:23).

But not now! For, one by one, men and women with Christian knowledge of the Risen Christ have appropriated them triumphantly, as you and I do today, in the light of Eastertide: "**I know that my Redeemer liveth!**" "If Christ be not risen", said Paul, whilst many who had been through the historic Easter occurrences were still living, "then is our preaching vain, and your faith is also vain" (1 Corinthians 15:14; A.V.).

I wonder where that prized autograph book, with its striking entry, is today? I don't know – but it doesn't matter. *Countless numbers of us carry its Easter certainty in our hearts*! *God be praised*!

Sharing Surprises

Working and Wondering

Now the Spring of souls has come,
Christ has burst His prison,
and from three days' sleep in death,
as a sun has risen;
all the winter of our sins,
long and dark, is flying
from His light, to Whom we give
laud and praise undying.

John of Damascus, A.D. 754

"*Expect surprises!*" says Dr George Morrison. "Have an open eye. Believe that there are more things in heaven and earth than have been dreamed of in your philosophies. And then, when common actions are irradiated, and common lives flash into moral glories, when the mysteries of Life, and Love, and Death so baffle us that we can only say with Paul, 'We know in part' – we shall be nearer the spirit of Jesus, than we dreamed."

The Great Surprise of the empty Tomb on the world's first Easter Morn, *is with us yet*! Luke's Gospel, which records the walk of the two dispirited followers to Emmaus, would attach it like a shining pendant to their grief. "Our own hope", said they, "was that He would be the Redeemer . . . but He is dead; and that is three days ago! *Though some women of our number gave us a surprise!*" (Luke 24:21,22; Moffatt).

R.F.S.

One Needs to Know

O sons and daughters, let us sing!
the King of Heaven, the glorious King,
o'er Death today, rose triumphing.
  Alleluia!

Jean Tisserand, A.D. 1494

Love's redeeming work is done;
fought the fight, the battle won;
vain the Stone, the Watch, the Seal;
Christ has burst the gates of Hell!

John Wesley

Death, in itself, is nothing; but we fear
To be we know not what, we know not where.

John Dryden

Jesus said: *"Father, into Thy hands I commit My spirit"*,
and with these words He died.

The New English Bible

Can you and I not do likewise? We can!

With Great Spirit

It was a fresh, sunny morning after rain. My public speaking obligations at an end, I started up my little car, and drove into Leicestershire having no hint of the surprise that would await me after I left the major road! Years before, and far away on our side of the world, I had read of rural Staunton and its famous church, and had memorized its inscription, paying tribute to its builder three hundred years earlier, during the grim days of the Civil War.

Now, here it was:

> In the yeare 1653, when all things sacred were throughout ye nation either demolished or profaned, Sir Robert Shirley, Barronet, founded this church; whose singular praise it is to have done *the best of things in ye worst times and hoped them in the most callamitous.*

I liked that! And its words, and shining truth, had walked up and down in my mind, since first I heard of it! And here it was, in actuality!

In a few moments, the ageing master of Staunton Hall, nearby, had ceased what he was doing in the garden, and was inviting me in "to a cup of tea". That, together with the talk that accompanied it, I shall never forget! My host had just acquired a *new bell-rope for distant Bottesford church*!

"But why," I asked, "should Staunton pay for a

With Great Spirit

bell-rope for Bottesford?" With a brightening of the eye, he explained. An ancestor received the lands of Staunton, from the standard-bearer of William the Conqueror, on one condition. Seven miles distant across country stands Belvoir Castle – and in between, Bottesford church! Whenever the reigning monarch comes to the castle, a flag is flown, and Staunton of Staunton must ride over with a golden key.

"But the mists may be down," explained my host. "Or it may be night – then, instead of a flag being run up, *a bell is rung*! It is heard at Bottesford church, and the tenor bell of Bottesford is rung; and finally, we get the call here at Staunton!" (And I was allowed to examine a piece of the discarded rope!)

But above all, to me it was *the deed* of Sir Robert Shirley, who there, where we stood at that moment, had done "the best of things in ye worst times", that rejoiced my heart. *For there is room for deeds embracing that glorious spirit, in every part of the world, in every age*!

All too often, we ordinary folk, concerned for better things in our commonly shared events, are content to delay in the doing of them, until all things are propitious! Or as some of us say, "till things look up"! And when that doesn't *soon* eventuate, we embrace the excuse for doing nothing at all!

That is not the secret of progress! *The Kingdom of God* will never come that way on this Earth, where He has set us to live. We need Sir Robert Shirley's spirit! And now!

Sharing Surprises

Working and Wondering

Because in tender majesty
Thou cam'st to earth, nor stayed till we,
Poor sinners, stumbled up to Thee,
I thank my God.

Because the Saviour of us all
Lay with the cattle in the stall,
Because the great came to the small,
I thank my God.

Because the Eternal Infinite
Was once that little naked Mite,
Because – O Love of Christmas night,
I thank my God!

                                    Padre G.A. Studdert-Kennedy

Sharing this same Earth – this Exultation, Adoration – Henry Ward Beecher exclaimed: "All the bells that God has put into my belfry shall ring!" Many's the time you've felt like that, I'm sure! *And what did you do?*

One choice Christian spirit, Abbie Graham, limited for words, says:

> As I watch the Christmas candles burn, I see in them a symbol of the great Love which dipped a lustrous Spirit into human form, that the world in

With Great Spirit

its darkness might be illuminated, and made beautiful.

What homes, parts, and places have you knowledge of – where this Christmas has been fully received?
And what personalities?

PRAYER

Gracious God, Giver of all Good, I adore Thee! I rejoice in the New Testament record of Thy glorious Love, shared with us Earth dwellers! For all dear ones, who have experienced a share in it! For all who journey still, with unwearying steps, and radiant faces!

Grant Thy special grace to all tending little children. Show us how to make room for the spirit of Christmas in our hearts, and homes, all the year through.

This is too much for us to attempt alone. Love us – forgive us – and let us be aware of Thy lasting Presence – as we go on our way. Deliver us from ever questioning Your Love, and grant us your continual wondrous keeping.

Give us courage to triumph in the hard places; practical helpfulness to share, with those we come across, where life hurts. In Christ's Name, we humbly fashion this prayer. Amen.

R.F.S.

The Best of Things

I've never thought that totally depressing reports in the press do much for us newspaper readers. Nor do I agree that wholly "gladsome tidings" would serve us any better. Again and again, in mixed company, I find the subject crops up. Such an attitude, I feel, is childish. Indeed, Arthur Mee experimented with the practicality of such a judgement. You remember his *Children's Newspaper* perhaps. I took it myself, for as long as it lasted - but it didn't last!

We will want to spare children as many "rough edges" as we can, but they can't hope to go through adulthood like that. "Money", "greed", "status", "sex", "speed", and "violence" do seem to get too big a share of public notice, I admit; but would ignoring them altogether help us? We've got to be adult. But that doesn't mean that we can't lay hold of opportunities, or deliberately make them, for some of life's "best of things".

You can't read the New Testament as regularly as your newspaper, and not realize "the adult costliness of life" that Christ knew. He played with the children – but not all the time. How adult He was! What choices He had to make! What values he had to embrace!

I'm thinking of some of the happiest days my friend Rene and I, with haversacks, sticks and walking shoes, spent in the south of England, going out

The Best of Things

from the unforgettable little thatched cottage village of Selworthy – all thanks to Sir Thomas Acland who in a very grim time, exercised a very adult, Christian choice, *"when the papers were carrying news of U-boats and of Ypres and heartbreaking casualty lists!"*

What a time it was, to do what he did! And it's only lately that the poet, Patricia Beer, writing a handsome book for The National Trust, called *Wessex*, used those very words to cover that glorious undertaking, which enabled Rene and me to walk high up there, over the moors, as have countless others. The National Trust's official record is as excited and grateful to record the name of that good man of our lifetime, Sir Thomas Acland, *"whose forethought and generosity preserved for them one of the most beautiful pieces of wild country to be found in England"*.

And so *great* an area, as I will always remember before God, when I think of it in this Earth, that He fashioned for us to share!

I have read many of Poet Patricia's poems; and her prose here pleases me as much. Not forgetting the glorious photographs – quickening my memory – furnished by her gifted photographic colleague, Fay Godwin!

Sharing Surprises

Working and Wondering

Gracious Lord, I bless Thee for every "surprise" that is mine, that stirs my spirit, to things of self-forgetting Love.

For the privilege of sharing with others, in good times and ill. Open my heart, I pray Thee, and my hands to share. Amen.

R.F.S.

> The Master was a man Who knew
>   The feel of rain, the touch of dew,
> The mystic kiss of midnight air
>   Upon His face upraised in prayer.
>
> His feet were stained in dusty ways,
>   His cheeks were brown as Autumn days;
> His skin, it had the look of One
>   Who travelled under wind and sun!

Anon

A HYMN
> For the beauty of the earth,
>   For the beauty of the skies,
> For the Love which from our birth,
>   Over and around us lies,
>   *Gracious God, to Thee we raise*
>   *This our sacrifice of praise!*

The Best of Things

For the beauty of each hour
  Of the day and of the night,
Hill and vale, and tree and flower,
  Sun and moon, and stars of light,
    Gracious God, to Thee we raise,
    This our sacrifice of praise!

Folliott S. Pierpoint, 1835-1917

MEDITATION
  Not here for high and holy things
  We render thanks to Thee,
  But for the common things of Earth,
  The purple pageantry
  Of dawning, and of dying days,
  The splendour of the sea,
  The royal robes of Autumn moors . . .

Padre G.A. Studdert-Kennedy

In His World

As long as I live, I shall offer God lasting praise that He made this world ROUND. I wouldn't have found it anything like such fun, if it had been any other shape.

As it is, it has been possible for me to be born on this *young side*, and go by ship, or air, eight times to the other side, stepping off anew into *old London*.

A while back, a little handful of type on the first page of my morning newspaper was enough to set me off to lay hold of *a surprise*. I could go this time to meet my Editor, by way of Charing Cross. It was a chilly February morning, but that made no difference. I had a good warm topcoat, and when I got to the bleak pavement, the "celebrant" I sought had on, as I knew he would, his bright wool jacket of red, and his blue trousers.

"How are things, this centenary celebration day?" I began, and got the cheerful answer I expected. Old Jim Pearse set about his job. I had never, since early childhood, had anyone polish my shoes, and it had been my mother who did them then, all that long time ago!

London's shoe-shine business, I learned, whilst the old man knelt there before me, the little sloping stand between us, had been started for the benefit of poor boys of the Ragged School. Numbers have gone up and down; when old Jim started, a "shine"

In His World

was rewarded with a penny, and it took six "shines" to buy a dinner. After that, any coppers he got had to be divided into three parts – a third for his own needs, a third for the Society, a third for an agreed bank account. All very modest – but protective! Mostly the boys worked in twos, as Jim and his colleague Alfred Harvey do today, making a bright patch on that bleak piece of pavement. "How long have you been at it?" I asked old Jim, as he knelt, drawing his polishing rag expertly and lovingly across my shoes, after he had laid aside his brushes and colour.

But there was, I felt, much more to it. "How long have you been at it?" I said again. "I began in nineteen hundred," he replied, "well over half the century."

"Now here we are," I thought to myself, "celebrating the *whole century*" – and that's no mean offering. For it is an offering – and I fell to wondering how many of us do as well?

And then, as I came away with that "centenary shine", to face the bustling world of London, I asked myself searchingly how constantly and thankfully do I bring my acceptance to those who offer me humble service, and with it adequate reward, and respect?

For world-round – in the sight of God our Father, *this is what I'm answerable for*!

Sharing Surprises

Working and Wondering

"That man who truly seeks to serve others," one has said, "must spend a good part of his time on his knees."

The man who said it may well have been thinking of the service of Prayer.

But you and I will know that there are other ways, as well. I will remember forever the one who served me on Charing Cross pavement.

PRAYER

Almighty and Wondrous God, Whose handiwork is seen in the world about us, we bless Thee for Thy presence revealed here in so many glorious ways.

> You are the Thought beyond all thought,
> The Gift beyond our utmost prayer;
> no farthest reach where You are not,
> no height but we may find You there.
>
> Elizabeth Havens Burrowes

PRAYER

O Lord, of all lowly service here, grant us Love and respect, knowledge, and patience.

Quicken all, and sustain those set on dependability throughout the passing years.

From age to age, with the sharing of common interests, and deeds, men and women have helped their neighbours. Teach us the joy of steady satisfaction.

In His World

Support us in our homes, our schools, and churches – and save us in private and public places. Thou hast set us in this world full of colour and variety.
Grant us together, generosity, integrity and love. Amen.

R.F.S.

Certain thoughts alone, are prayers. There are moments, when, whatever the attitude of the body, the soul is on its knees.

Victor Hugo

The pathway of the saints is paved with ever fresh beginnings . . .
Every day is a day of Creation, every Spring is a creative Spring.
God is eternally a Creator.

"One of the delightful things going to happen upon the Day of Judgement," says Alistair Maclean in *High Country*, "is that we shall get to know God's successful men and women. There will be *surprises*!"

ACKNOWLEDGEMENTS

The author acknowledges with gratitude the use of the following material:

John Baillie, *Christian Devotion*, Oxford University Press 1962, p.17

"O God, Source of all light", poem by Cecil Hunt

"The God Who had such heart for us", poem by Robert Farren

"It was a man like me", poem by the Rev. James Asa Johnson

"And sitting down, they watched Him there", G.A. Studdert-Kennedy, *Poems*, Hodder & Stoughton

"It is a sun-baked road", poem by my late dear friend Teresa Hooley

"I saw Him once", poem by Thomas Curtis Clark

"Because in tender majesty", G.A. Studdert-Kennedy, *Poems*, Hodder & Stoughton

Quotations from untraced sources will be acknowledged in any reprint if the author receives further information about them, but so far efforts to trace copyright holders have proved unsuccessful.

Also available in Fount Paperbacks

BIOGRAPHIES

Bonhoeffer
Eberhard Bethge

"Will surely stand as the definitive and authoritative work on the subject . . . more than just a fascinating exploration of a hero of our time. It is, as well, a spiritual experience."

Malcolm Muggeridge, The Observer

A Backdoor to Heaven
Lionel Blue

". . . an extraordinary man . . . an extraordinary autobiography . . . not to be missed."

The Tablet

Audacity to Believe
Sheila Cassidy

A "humorous, warm, moving, terrifying and enormously readable . . . account of one woman's struggle to understand what Christian obedience demands . . ." in South America.

The Baptist Times

Thomas More
Richard Marius

"A biography as good as this one – uncluttered, brightly written, yet scrupulous in its use of sources – brings a complex man out of romantic legend and puts him squarely in the clear light of history."

Times Educational Supplement

Also available in Fount Paperbacks

The Mind of St Paul
WILLIAM BARCLAY

'There is a deceptive simplicity about this fine exposition of Pauline thought at once popular and deeply theological. The Hebrew and Greek backgrounds are described and all the main themes are lightly but fully treated.' *The Yorkshire Post*

The Plain Man Looks at the Beatitudes
WILLIAM BARCLAY

'. . . the author's easy style should render it . . . valuable and acceptable to the ordinary reader.' *Church Times*

The Plain Man Looks at the Lord's Prayer
WILLIAM BARCLAY

Professor Barclay shows how this prayer that Jesus gave to his disciples is at once a summary of Christian teaching and a pattern for all prayers.

The Plain Man's Guide to Ethics
WILLIAM BARCLAY

The author demonstrates beyond all possible doubt that the Ten Commandments are the most relevant document in the world today and are totally related to mankind's capacity to live and make sense of it all within a Christian context.

Ethics in a Permissive Society
WILLIAM BARCLAY

How do we as Christians deal with such problems as drug taking, the 'pill', alcohol, morality of all kinds, in a society whose members are often ignorant of the Church's teaching? Professor Barclay approaches a difficult and vexed question with his usual humanity and clarity, asking what Christ himself would say or do in our world today.

Fount Paperbacks

Fount is one of the leading paperback publishers of religious books and below are some of its recent titles.

- ☐ THROUGH SEASONS OF THE HEART John Powell £4.95
- ☐ WORDS OF LIFE FROM JOHN THE BELOVED Frances Hogan £2.95
- ☐ MEISTER ECKHART Ursula Fleming £2.95
- ☐ CHASING THE WILD GOOSE Ron Ferguson £2.95
- ☐ A GOOD HARVEST Rita Snowden £2.50
- ☐ UNFINISHED ENCOUNTER Bob Whyte £5.95
- ☐ FIRST STEPS IN PRAYER Jean-Marie Lustiger £2.95
- ☐ IF THIS IS TREASON Allan Boesak £2.95
- ☐ RECLAIMING THE CHURCH Robin Greenwood £2.95
- ☐ GOD WITHIN US John Wijngaards £2.95
- ☐ GOD'S WORLD Trevor Huddleston £2.95
- ☐ A CALL TO WITNESS Oliver McTernan £2.95
- ☐ GOODNIGHT LORD Georgette Butcher £2.95
- ☐ FOR GOD'S SAKE Donald Reeves £3.50
- ☐ GROWING OLDER Una Kroll £2.95
- ☐ THROUGH THE YEAR WITH FRANCIS OF ASSISI Murray Bodo £2.95

All Fount Paperbacks are available at your bookshop or newsagent, or they can be ordered by post from Fount Paperbacks, Cash Sales Department, G.P.O. Box 29, Douglas, Isle of Man. Please send purchase price plus 22p per book, maximum postage £3. Customers outside the UK send purchase price, plus 22p per book. Cheque, postal order or money order. No currency.

NAME (Block letters) _____

ADDRESS _____

_____

_____

While every effort is made to keep prices low, it is sometimes necessary to increase them at short notice. Fount Paperbacks reserve the right to show new retail prices on covers which may differ from those previously advertised in the text or elsewhere.